HOW TO
CAPTURE
LIVE AUTHORS

and Bring Them
To Your Schools

HOW TO CAPTURE

C. S. Adler

William Sleator

Dana Brookins

William MacKellar

and Bring Them

LIVE AUTHORS

Mary Calhoun

David Harrison

Robert Burch

Patricia Calvert

To Your Schools

**practical and innovative ways
to schedule authors for
Author-in-Residence Programs,
Children's Literature Festivals
and Young Authors' Days**

**WRITTEN
and
ILLUSTRATED
by**

David Melton

LANDMARK EDITIONS, INC.
Kansas City, Missouri

PHOTOGRAPHIC CREDITS

The Children's Literature Festival
Central Missouri State University
Warrensburg, Missouri

James Gilbert

The Children's Literature Festival
of the Ozarks
Springfield, Missouri

Second Edition

International Standard Book Number: 0-933849-03-6

Library of Congress Catalog Card Number: 85-81416

First Edition, First Printing, March, 1986

Landmark Editions, Inc.
1420 Kansas Avenue
Kansas City, Missouri 64127
(816) 241-4919

Printed in the United States of America

To PHILIP A. SADLER,
OPHELIA GILBERT,
and
all of the wonderful
teachers and librarians
who create
author-related programs
that offer students opportunities
to meet their favorite writers and illustrators.

Contents

CREATING THE LITERARY EVENT OF THE SCHOOL YEAR

SET THE TRAP, LOAD THE BAIT

$ $ DOLLARS AND SENSE $ $

"SOMEHOW IT ALL COMES TOGETHER"

DOUBLE PLEASURE, TRIPLE FUN!

Acknowledgments

No book is ever developed by one person alone — each one is an accumulation of information, drawn from various sources, experiences and influences. I cannot remember any previous books I've written having had so many contributions by so many people.

I am indebted to those hundreds of teachers and librarians who have created author-related programs, and who through the years have invited me to speak at these functions, providing me with a multitude of first-hand experiences in the *do's* and *don'ts* of program organization.

I appreciate the wonderful assistance from members of the International Reading Association and the Association of School Librarians who so generously furnished helpful information and suggestions about their programs.

I am grateful to the many published authors and illustrators who replied to my questionnaire with such candor, offering astute observations and insights. I am particularly gratified that so many of my colleagues allowed me to quote their professional opinions and personal thoughts on the subject of author-related school programs.

In the development of the manuscript, I deeply appreciate the splendid assistance and editing of Nancy Melton.

For the preparation and writing of a special section on media coverage, I am especially grateful to Rosemary Lumsden.

In the research and production phases, I appreciate the efforts of Philip A. Sadler, Ophelia Gilbert, Teresa Melton, Dr. Kaye Anderson, Dr. Glen Anderson, Marge Hagerty, Linda Hammer and Jack Berry, and my special thanks to the superb assistance of the staff of Uppercase, Inc.

To Robert Braden of Landmark Editions, Inc., I am profoundly grateful for his constant support and encouragement.

Introduction

Author Programs Benefit Students, and Teachers Too

More often than not, readers tend to hold authors in awe and place them on high pedestals. As a lifelong reader, I, too, have revered the authors of books I enjoyed and considered these persons to be as unapproachable as the gods on Mount Olympus.

After teaching a children's literature college course for a few semesters to prospective teachers and librarians, I became increasingly intrigued with the idea of personally meeting some of my literary idols. I acknowledge that in the beginning my actions were selfish and still continue to be.

When I had the idea of initiating a small Children's Literature Festival on the campus of Central Missouri State University in the Spring of 1969, I approached my good friend and the librarian of our laboratory school, Ophelia Gilbert, who gave me immediate support and valuable advice and assistance.

Our first festival was attended by only a few authors of children's books from the Kansas City area and the children in the laboratory school. Although it was little more than a "small literary tea," it was a great success. After a couple of successful festivals with local writers, I ventured to contact authors from other areas whom I wanted to meet.

During the next ten years, the event "exploded" into an annual four-day affair which is now attended by approximately 3,500 children and the teachers, librarians and parents who accompany them. They come from numerous elementary schools in Missouri and Kansas to meet twenty-five authors and illustrators who have national and international reputations.

Our first festival was held in one room. Now the entire education building is required to accommodate the busloads of excited children and enthusiastic adults. Two special lectures have been added for adults who are interested in literature for children and young adults.

The idea of introducing children to some of their favorite authors has become so popular that festivals, patterned after ours, are annual affairs at three other state universities in Missouri. Many librarians and teachers who attend our festival return to their own schools and arrange for author visits. Often they phone or write us for advice and "how-to" assistance in the promotion of author appearances. Even a good number of authors have returned home and become instrumental in promoting festivals in their own states.

Effective planning and conducting of festivals or author visitations in schools require teachers and librarians who love children and who realize that reading good books enriches the lives of their students. Those enlightened educators who develop author-related school programs reap the grand rewards of seeing children's faces glow with the happiness of reading good books and meeting the wonderful authors who have written them. And besides, these activities offer teachers and librarians opportunities to meet and greet their favorite authors too. On these occasions, everyone benefits — the children, the educators and the authors.

Responding to the Call

Growing numbers of requests for help have made me acutely aware of the expanding need for an informative handbook for teachers and librarians. Since David Melton has participated in a number of festivals and visited in numerous schools throughout the country, I believe he is the right person to write such a book. During his visits as an author, he has observed the various methods of conducting festivals and programs, consulted teachers and librarians regarding their schools' needs and expectations, and talked with his fellow au-

thors and illustrators about their experiences in meeting with children. He also knows how such activities can enhance the joy of reading in some children and awaken others to the fact that reading is fun. And he realizes such activities promote authors' careers, increase sales of their books, and often inspire them to write even more and better books for children.

If you are already sponsoring author-related school programs, this book may very well provide you with ways to improve and broaden the scope of your activities. If you are just beginning to initiate such programs, how fortunate you are to have discovered this book. So read, utilize, and enjoy!

— Philip A. Sadler
Co-Director,
Annual Children's Literature Festival
Associate Professor of Children's Literature
Central Missouri State University

Foreword

David Melton

Along Came Mr. Guthrie — To Be Captured by Student

The first time I captured an author, I was fifteen years old. A. B. Guthrie, Jr., was scheduled to speak at Drury College in my hometown of Springfield, Missouri, and our high school journalism teacher arranged for ten of her students to attend.

I could hardly wait to meet Mr. Guthrie. I had enjoyed his epic novel, THE WAY WEST, and thought it was one of the greatest books I had ever read. To add to my excitement, one line in Mr. Guthrie's biography mentioned that he had just completed the screenplay based on Jack Schaefer's SHANE, another one of the greatest books I had ever read. So I read both books again and started making a list of questions.

Although Mr. Guthrie was certainly worth the wait, he was not at all what I had expected. In my mind, I had envisioned he would look as brawny and burly as one of the heroes in his books. Instead, he was a very small man, neatly dressed in a gray suit, who looked more like an accountant or maybe a conservative college professor. His voice was smaller still. Even with amplification, we could barely hear him.

After he was introduced, he immediately told the audience that he was not a public speaker, so he would say only a few things about writing. Then he would answer our questions — a time I was happily anticipating since I had prepared and assembled three pages of notes. As I recall, he told us very little about writing. Instead, he related ways he had researched types of wagons and oxbows used during our nation's western expansion, all the while praising the spirit of the pioneers, trappers and traders. Everything he said was interesting, but eventually I began to realize that time for questions and answers was growing shorter and shorter.

With only five minutes remaining, he finally asked

if there were any questions. Hands were raised and he pointed to those of college students who occupied front rows in the center. He didn't even see mine. After three-questions-worth of answers, a teacher announced that the time was up and Mr. Guthrie had to leave immediately for the airport. And he was ushered out the side door.

Forgetting my teacher's instructions for our group to stay together at all times, I dashed to the back of the auditorium and ran outside, just in time to see Mr. Guthrie climb into the back seat of a waiting car and shut the door.

To this day, I still can't believe my sudden surge of brashness. I ran to the car and tapped on the window. As Mr. Guthrie rolled down the window, I waved my list in front of his face and said: "You told us you'd have time to answer questions, but I didn't get to ask any of mine."

He apologized, then said the only way he would be able to answer my questions would be for me to ride to the airport with him. I suspect he was no more surprised than I when I opened the door, stepped inside and sat down.

Although someone must have driven the car, I have no memory of anyone else being present. I started rattling off my questions and, one by one, Mr. Guthrie answered them. When we arrived at the airport, I stayed with him until he boarded the plane. It wasn't until the airplane left the ground that I finally realized I was AWOL from school and didn't have enough money for bus fare back to town. I didn't even have a nickel for the pay telephone and had to ask permission to call home from one of the airport offices. I had to wait for more than three hours until my father got off from work and could pick me up. I had some explaining to do to Dad that night and to my teacher the following day, but it was worth it.

Although Drury College had paid for Mr. Guthrie's visit, I was confident that I had been the one who captured the author. I suspect he knew it too.

What important questions did I pose to Mr. Guthrie? I have no idea. I have long since forgotten. However, I do remember Mr. Guthrie's face, the sound of his voice, and his very nice manner. And I have no doubt, while riding in the car with him, that I decided I, too, would someday write a book.

Mine was no idle vow. Some twenty-five years later, having had several books published, the tables were turned and as a guest author, I spoke to my first group of students. Since that event, I have been captured thousands of times, and I have loved meeting the students and still do!

"A Real Live Author!"

"I can't believe a real live author would come to our school!" exclaims a twelve-year-old girl.

And other students echo her sense of wonder and amazement:

"I never thought authors were really people!"

"You're the first famous person I've ever met!"

"Do you know Judy Blume and other famous writers?"

"Do you drive a Cadillac?"

"Are you rich?"

Any author who has spoken to students on a regular basis has experienced those comments hundreds of times. And unless the authors have become insensate to human emotions or immune to the starry-eyed innocence of children, upon hearing such statements, they probably feel hefty boosts to their egos and they are surely charmed.

Although I have spoken to thousands of young readers while participating in hundreds of author-related school programs throughout the country — Author-in-

Residence Programs, Young Authors' Days activities and Children's Literature Festivals — when I enter a school building and see the excited, expectant faces of students, I still sense an air of electricity and my spirits rise.

I am delighted when a student says: "Because I knew you were coming, I read my first book from cover to cover."

I am thrilled when a teacher remarks: "Some of my students read books that are two and three grade levels beyond anything they have ever read before."

And the statement which most pleases me is one I hear from many students: "Because of your visit to my school, I have decided to become a writer!"

While presenting school programs, I have also had opportunities to meet some of the most dedicated educators in the world — those teachers, librarians and principals who selflessly expend enormous amounts of energy to organize programs which provide students with the enriching experiences of meeting live authors.

The majority of programs are splendidly organized, the students are well prepared, and the hospitality is most cordial — all of which provided me with some of my fondest memories.

Teachers, Librarians and Authors Offer Assistance

Before beginning this book, I wrote to a number of librarians and teachers nationwide who had developed author-related programs. Many responded by sending valuable information. I also sent questionnaires to more than one hundred authors who speak regularly at school functions. They also responded generously by sending me a wealth of information and ideas from which to draw.

I have tried to prepare the book's format as conversationally as possible. It is not intended to be a one-sided narrative, but a friendly dialogue between people who are mutually eager to provide students with the unique and enriching opportunities of meeting their favorite authors and illustrators. Through this writing I hope to be one small, but effective, voice in encouraging teachers and librarians to develop more and better author-related school programs.

And now, on to the capture of live authors!

— David Melton

A Memorable Experience

My most memorable author's visit was to Jefferson City, Missouri. I'm sure nothing will ever be as ideal. Genevieve O'Halloran, Coordinator of Elementary School Libraries, wrote to tell me that I was "far and away their first author choice" as a candidate to visit their schools and asked if I'd be interested if they could get a grant to cover my travel and other expenses. Flattered, I said, "Yes," and six months later, after a great deal of careful organization by Genevieve and her staff, I arrived.

I expected to be spending two or three evenings alone in a motel, but that dismal expectation never materialized. My hostess offered me companionship during dinner and breakfast, plus a gala party the next evening, attended by the mayor who gave me a certificate acclaiming me "Queen for a Day in Jeff City."

The children in the four presentations I made in schools on each of my two days there were familiar with my books, full of interesting questions and eager to have me sign copies of books they had bought. Would you believe that each school also presented me with a memento of my trip? I received a quick-stitched, framed representation of their favorite books of mine, photograph scrapbooks and a pillow with the children's names. I keep them in my office, of course.

The final filip came when my plane for the next leg of my trip was canceled and I was stranded in an isolated little airport to be rescued by Pat Behler of the state library. She drove me two-and-one-half hours to my next destination and claimed it was no bother at all. I did get paid in money, but the warmth and hospitality I received was worth much more.

— C. S. Adler, author of
    FOOTSTEPS ON THE STAIRS

Barbara Robinson

1

CREATING THE LITERARY EVENT OF THE SCHOOL YEAR

Designing and Improving Programs

Each year thousands of schools throughout the country invite authors and illustrators to speak to classes of students. While it is a good idea, it is hardly a new one. From the time materials were first published, authors have been asked to speak to political, educational and secular groups. As Socrates was a writer, he was also a teacher and a guest speaker. So it has been with most writers of fact and fiction — once their writings are published, they are asked to stand before audiences to instruct, inform and/or entertain. In recent years, with greater amounts of material being written and published for children and young adults, more and more authors are asked to speak to younger groups.

Creating Wonderful Experiences for Young Readers

Because the effective use of language in receiving and expressing ideas and information is a predominant goal of educators, it is easy to see why authors are of vital interest in educational settings. The prime function of authors is to skillfully transform thought processes into written language.

Their ability to write stories fascinates us. Rarely do any of us finish a good book without wishing that we could talk with the author and ask him or her **how** and **why** the book was created and **what** made the writer choose a particular subject. I would give my eye teeth for five minutes with Mark Twain, or William Shakespeare, or Allen Drury, or Majorie Kinnan Rawlings, or any number of brilliant writers of books whom I have admired. And I'm sure many of you would too.

Enormous benefits are reaped from having an author visit your school, speak to students, and answer their questions. Students and teachers gain insights into written materials. For the first time, many students experi-

— James Stevenson,
author and illustrator of
WHAT'S UNDER MY BED?

— Harold Keith, author of
RIFLES FOR WATIE

A Delightful Visit

I was invited to talk to the sixth grade of a local school where the teacher had read my latest book aloud to his class. I was greeted at the school entrance by one of the students, dressed in her best.

Classroom chairs were arranged in a circle, and we had a wonderful discussion based on the ideas and contents of the book, which were familiar to all the children. Little time was spent on the stereotype questions (How many books have you written? How long does it take to write a book?).

I believe this session went well because the teacher had thoroughly prepared for my visit. By his reading and their prior discussions, he had aroused the interest of the children in the theme of the book and in the writing process.

As a parting gift, the children presented me with a potted azalea.

— Marian Potter, author of
BLATHERSKITE

ence a personal relationship with reading. And those students and teachers who desire to write, receive inspiration and valuable information.

If the idea of bringing your favorite authors into your schools interests you, you are about to have a wonderful time, because we are going to explore ways of setting up and improving exciting programs that will delight the students, teachers, librarians, parents and citizens of your community.

Initiating Author-Related Programs

How do we begin to initiate an author-related program in our school?

You begin with the idea. Often that idea comes from one or two teachers or librarians who feel the importance of offering students opportunities to meet authors and illustrators.

How Do We Gain the Support of the Administration?

It's a matter of priorities. In school systems where top priority is placed on getting students personally involved with the reading process, support is readily available and given for such programs.

*If you like, you may show these pages
to your principal and school superintendent.*

By their deeds shall ye know them!

One can **talk** about the importance of reading until the Moon turns to green cheese, but only those schools which **actively initiate** vital programs reveal their true interest and good intent.

In school systems where sports are of major interest to the community, we find monumental structures for stadiums and gymnasiums. In systems where reading is sincerely considered, we find fully stocked libraries located in the center of activities.

In a school where the library is crammed into a makeshift closet and where the librarian has to go begging for books, it is absurd to try to persuade anyone that reading or quality education is a top priority. Such a suggestion is no more than meaningless rhetoric.

When should we present the idea to the principal?

Not until you know what type of program you are going to propose and what it will cost. Too many ideas are squelched before they have a chance to succeed because they are not properly organized and presented.

By the way, I don't wish to paint the picture that all school principals are obstacles to overcome, for such is rarely the case. Many author-related programs are initiated **by principals** to teachers and librarians, instead of the other way around. Most principals and administrators respond favorably when teachers offer a good idea and present it well.

How many teachers should be on the committee?

At the start, three people are better than two because three people can easily demonstrate a quorum of opinion and a united front. If the school librarian becomes the fourth person in the group, better still. Because the school librarian is accustomed to ordering books and is more apt to be acquainted with information from publishers and distributors, he or she should prove to be of enormous help throughout the project.

What will school administrators want to know?

Administrators are going to be interested in four major factors:

1. What type of program are you planning?

2. How will the program benefit the students, teachers, school and community?

3. What will the program cost?

4. How can the program be financed?

These are proper considerations. The better you are able to answer these questions, the better are your chances of initiating an author-related program in your school.

While the enthusiast within me would rather plunge headlong into planning the event and worry about the cost later, the realist knows full well that no matter how worthwhile a project may be or how many people's lives it enhances, in order to initiate a new program or expand an existing one, you must first design a working plan, propose methods of finance, and be prepared to answer pertinent questions.

So your committee needs to formulate and coordinate the following:

- Design the best type of program for your school;

- Analyze the program's benefits to your students, teachers, school and community;

- Estimate the cost; and

- Investigate methods of financing.

How do we select the proper program for our school?

You and your committee should review various types of programs that have been successfully developed in other schools, then decide which one best fits the needs of your school or district.

The Basic Types of Author-Related Programs

There are four basic types of author-related programs:

1. **Visiting Author**

2. **Author-in-Residence**

3. **Young Authors' Days**

4. **Children's Literature Festivals**

Visiting Author Programs

The visiting author program is the easiest to arrange. Quite simply, an author is invited to come to your school to speak to individual classes or to joint sessions.

Warm and Wonderful Responses to Program

At a regional workshop for elementary and junior high students, the kids had read my books and discussed them in class. They came prepared with pertinent questions. Letters had gone home to the parents and many had sent checks so their children could buy books. Some parents attended the session and asked logical questions. All this promotes more interest in reading and in authors — also in student writing.

— Dorothy Francis, author of
CAPTAIN MORGANA MASON

— Joan Lowery Nixon, author of
THE GHOSTS OF NOW

— Mildred D. Taylor, author of
ROLL OF THUNDER,
HEAR MY CRY

Who's on First — What's on Second

Seven other speakers and I were invited to an awards ceremony, each of us thinking we were the only one and with one-and-one-half-hour talks prepared. None of us need have worried — the hostess took up most of the time herself with us as audience.

— Berniece Rabe, author of
NAOMI

Author-in-Residence Programs

An author is invited to visit a school for a longer period of time to work directly with the students and teachers on writing or creative projects. Some colleges and universities set up Author-in-Residence positions for professional writers. The writer is paid a salary while working on an original book, and he or she is expected to teach one or more classes during a semester and to conduct special seminars or workshops. Authors are sometimes hired for shorter periods of time as Authors-in-Residence for high schools and lower grades, but these occasions are rare.

It should be noted that some schools set up Visiting Author Programs and title them "Author-in-Residence Programs." However, one must stretch the imagination to conclude that a few nights' stay in a local hotel or motel establishes a residence. In such cases, the school is really sponsoring an extended Visiting Author Program or a mini-workshop.

Young Authors' Day Programs

Young Authors' Days are usually sponsored and organized by local or regional councils of the International Reading Association and ordinarily involve more than just one day of author-related programs.

Months prior to the event, members of the council urge teachers to encourage their students to write, and sometimes illustrate, special creative projects. Many groups have students write and illustrate complete books, then show them how to assemble and bind the pages. Some groups allow students to submit short stories, essays, poems, and so on. The best entries are selected from different age categories and printed in an anthology of students' works. Instead of publishing anthologies, other groups prefer to simply present Awards of Achievement.

To celebrate the completion of student projects, a special day of activities is scheduled. Authors are invited to speak, special workshops are conducted, and awards are presented to student writers.

Children's Literature Festivals

Children's Literature Festivals are also exciting! In full swing, they combine the atmospheres of a field trip, a convention, a gala celebration and a picnic.

One of the most energetic and best-planned festivals is held each spring at Central Missouri State University in Warrensburg. About eighteen years ago, Philip Sadler, Associate Professor of Children's Literature, and Ophelia Gilbert, Children's Librarian, invited four regional authors to speak to some 300 students in the campus laboratory school. Within ten years, the festival grew to staggering proportions. Now as many as twenty-five authors participate, and more than 3,500 children and teachers arrive in buses, cars and vans.

While some teachers may enroll their total classrooms, others set qualifying standards for students to meet before they are allowed to attend the festival, such as reading a certain number of books in a given period of time, or maintaining a particular grade average, or writing a paper expressing why they would like to meet an author, and so on.

Throughout the day, the groups are assigned to sessions with various authors. The festival schedule is designed so that all students have the opportunity to enjoy sessions conducted by six different authors.

The festival also includes a dinner that evening for adults only so the guest speaker can discuss his or her work and recent trends in children's literature. The following day offers a more informal meet-the-author day for teachers, librarians and interested adults who have the opportunity to meet and talk with the individual authors and to hear a guest speaker at a luncheon.

I think Mr. Sadler and Ms. Gilbert have been very wise in separating the functions for children from those for adults, because it allows guest speakers to direct their information to each specific audience.

Variations of the Four Basic Themes

Most other programs are simply variations of these four themes. Some schools have authors visit for a day, speak to several classes and conduct mini-workshops, and regard this approach as an Author-in-Residence Program. Other schools retain several authors to speak to classes and call the events Children's Literature Festivals or Conferences, and so on.

Which type of program is the easiest to initiate and development?

There is no doubt that the Visiting Author Program is the easiest because sessions are usually scheduled within one building and less preparation is involved. Many schools have started with this kind of program, then branched out to include various types of workshops and seminars. Some Visiting Author Programs expand to include several schools. Others eventually become districtwide activities.

Which type of program is best?

That's like asking: "Which is best — steak or lobster?" Both are nourishing and both are delicious. It depends on your taste, the price of the meal, and the size of your pocketbook.

Advantages and Disadvantages of the Four Types of Programs

All four types of programs share a common advantage — they offer students the opportunity to meet and hear an author speak.

But each type of program also has distinct advantages and disadvantages.

Visiting Author Programs

Advantages

- Students are allowed personal contact with the author who visits them in their own classrooms. Sometimes two classes meet in one classroom for economy's sake. Many authors prefer to meet students who are in their own surroundings. In such a close environment, the author does not have to speak via electronic amplification, but can react to individuals, face-to-face.

- Students are not required to achieve some task in order to attend. I have known of a number of children who are unable to read twenty or so books or who cannot write a complete story before an author's arrival, but they are so turned on by meeting the author that they read all of the author's books and start to write stories of their own.

A Happy Blend

During the course of my career as participant in book fairs, etc., one that I have particularly enjoyed was the Children's Literature Festival at Central Missouri State University in Warrensburg, directed by Philip Sadler.

Why? Hmmmm. It was a happy blend of compatible authors who respected each other's work, and who enjoyed each other's company and the warm, hospitable hosting. I imagine the children and teachers also appreciated this warm, comfortable environment.

There was plenty of advance notice, clear planning, accurate information gathered and dispensed, plenty of publicity, and enthusiastic participation by huge numbers of school children and teachers.

— Betty Horvath, author of
NOT ENOUGH INDIANS

— Glen Rounds,
author and illustrator of
OL' PAUL,
THE MIGHTY LOGGER

Unwelcomed Surprises

Once I flew to a midwestern town for two and one-half days in the schools. My plane landed at night, and the drive to the actual destination was another forty-five minutes. During the drive, the coordinator said offhandedly that she had neglected to make my reservation at a motel, so I was to be housed in the home of the school superintendent. She didn't even ask, "Is that all right?"

I was stuffed in a teenager's room. It was a one-bathroom situation. There was no place to relax alone in the evenings. And the house was located in an isolated neighborhood where there was no place for me to walk to in the late afternoon.

The coordinator scheduled me in fourteen schools in the two-and-one-half-day period, and the children weren't very well prepared. The only pleasant part of the visit was the company of retired teachers who drove me around.

My paycheck was not ready — I was told it would be mailed. After two or three weeks, I inquired about it and received a really nasty letter from the coordinator, saying it had been mailed. No paycheck arrived. A week later I phoned, and after a lot of confusion, the office discovered the check had been mailed to a bookbinder — Bound-To-Stay-Bound — who happened to have bound one of my books. Eventually I got a check but no thank-you note for my efforts.

The coordinator also gave me nervous palpitations about missing my plane home because she dallied so about getting me to the airport.

I will never go there again!

— Mary Calhoun, author of
the KATIE JOHN series

Disadvantages

- The limited time of a one-day visit may tempt coordinators to divide the author's time into too many segments. Such overscheduling spreads the visitor too thin to allow sufficient time with each group. Or the author has to speak to an auditorium filled with students where the quality of personal contact is lessened.

Author-in-Residence Programs

Advantages

- The longer period of time offers excellent opportunities for teachers and students to become better acquainted with the published author and his or her work.

- Allows students to receive individual instruction from a published author.

- Offers students professional evaluations of their work.

- Provides maximum motivation and information.

Disadvantages

- Not all authors are good teachers. Even the best of writers may be unable to organize lesson plans and verbalize proper instructions.

- The best workshops demand that an author reads the students' works in order to offer proper suggestions. However, some authors, although willing to instruct, do not want to commit themselves to reading the work of so many students.

- Because the author spends more time with each class and has contact with fewer students, the cost per student can be quite expensive. Most schools can't afford to bring in an author for such an extended period of time to work only with a select few teachers and students.

Young Authors' Day Programs

Advantages

- Students must have written a work of merit in order to participate.
- Participating students receive recognition for their achievements.
- Selected works of students are either published or placed on public display.

Disadvantages

- Those students whose works have not been selected miss the opportunity to meet and hear the authors and illustrators speak.

Children's Literature Festivals

Advantages

- Students have the chance to meet several authors and to hear them speak.

- Other than the expense of transporting students to and from the event, the cost per student is usually quite economical.

Disadvantages

- Sometimes the groups are so large that personal contact with the authors is extremely limited.

- In the presence of so many people and in a strange environment, some students become intimidated and are hesitant to ask questions.

- Not all students may be allowed to attend, which eliminates the opportunity for some underachievers to take part in such a fine motivating experience.

Should we strictly adhere to the format of one of the four types of programs?

Instead of being stymied by rigid guidelines, I hope you will pick and choose and mix and match as you see fit.

The International Reading Association has appointed a Young Authors' Day Conference Committee to develop guidelines for their programs. In a recent conversation, the National Chairperson, Pat Henry, said she hoped when the guidelines are completed that they are not so stringent as to stifle the creativity of program coordinators. I certainly agree. I would hate to see schools wind up with "Kentucky Fried" programs.

Of the hundreds of programs in which I have participated, no two have been alike. Even the most successful ones have been very different from each other. Every program has a direction and an energy all its own. I urge you to be innovative in your approach.

When is the best time of year to schedule author-related programs?

I am asked to speak at more school programs during the spring months — March, April and May. However, if I were a teacher who wanted to take full advantage of accelerating student interest in reading, I would schedule programs as early in the school year as possible — September, October or November.

Is it best to schedule an author before or after students develop writing projects?

There are advantages in both.

Having an author at the beginning of a writing project can certainly be of benefit to both teachers and students. The author can offer many insights into selecting an idea, methods of approach, writing processes, the importance of editing, and how to complete a manuscript. These sessions can be highly informative and motivating.

Engaging authors to speak at the conclusion of a writing project can also provide incentives and motivation for students. When young people know someone special will see their achievements, they often put forth their finest efforts. Also, having been involved with writing, editing, and completing a manuscript of their own may prepare students to develop better questions.

Perhaps in the best of all possible worlds, you would be allowed to invite one author to speak to classes as a kick-off for a creative writing

Before Instead of After

When the emphasis is on writing, I wish the schools would schedule me at the opening of the year, rather than at its end.

— Mary Francis Shura, author of MISTER WOLF AND ME

Quantity Versus Quality

Keep literary standards high. I am rabid about the quality and quantity of nonbooks being published. I don't like to see little kids conned into thinking that almost any old combination of words and pictures constitutes a real, genuine, worthwhile reading experience.

For that matter, I don't like to see great big grown-ups conned by nonbooks, either, but at least they should be big enough to know better.

— Betty Horvath, author of
NOT ENOUGH INDIANS

— Gary Paulsen, author of
WINTERKILL

project and another one to speak at the event celebrating the students' efforts.

Always Consider Your Main Purpose for Having an Author-Related Program

If you want your program to accelerate your students' interest in reading, then emphasis should be placed on reading.

If you want your program to also inform and motivate your students to write, then you should schedule it to correspond with special writing projects.

Going Public

Although the public relations factor should not be a prime consideration in scheduling such programs, if these programs are conducted properly, they can bring additional support for the schools from parents and the community. When parents see students become more interested, even excited, about reading and eager to meet a guest author, they know the teachers and administrators of their school are expending extra effort to provide better quality education and more enriching experiences.

If I were a principal, school librarian or teacher who wanted to send a message to parents and the community that my main interest was to encourage and elevate the reading and writing skills of our students, I can think of no better way of proclaiming such goals than by initiating and maintaining an annual literary event.

If you already have such a program, through the course of these pages you may discover exciting ways of improving and broadening its scope.

If you are about to initiate a new program, you have the opportunity to begin from scratch and utilize many of the suggestions presented and discussed.

Either way, you have the wherewithal to create events that will affect the lives of your students in positive ways and provide everyone involved with experiences to share and remember for the rest of their lives.

Having a Wonderful Time!

Since I am just back from one appearance which left me feeling very UP, let me use it as an example for a successful trip.

It was a trip to Portland, Oregon, and was initiated by a personal letter from a child, asking if I could visit her school. Enclosed was a cover letter from the school librarian, confirming the invitation.

I responded to the child's questions about my books, and also wrote a letter to the librarian, indicating my possible availability for a visit and telling her what the cost (honorarium plus expenses) would be. In addition, I told her what I was willing to do for that price. (That's an important point, I think. They can't read your mind. You can't blame them for wanting to get their money's worth. But sometimes they take advantage. Now I make clear in advance what I am willing — and able — to do.)

There followed a period of correspondence between me and the librarian and several phone calls from her to me as well. She asked specific questions: Would I like, perhaps, to stay in her home, instead of a hotel? (She made clear that she had no dogs or noisy children.) Would I mind autographing paperback books as well as hardcover? Would I like to go sight seeing during my stay? And so on. The specific questions were perhaps not as important as the general concept of adequate communication. By the time I got on the plane to Oregon, I knew *exactly* what I would be doing while I was there, and she knew *exactly* what to expect from me.

My prepaid tickets were sent to me and followed up by a phone call to confirm that I had received them. A phone call two days before I left Boston gave me an idea of the kind of weather to expect.

I was met at the Portland Airport. I did — having agreed in advance — stay in a private home, and no effort was spared to make my stay there comfortable. There were fresh flowers in my room, and I was given adequate time to be alone (since I had made it clear in advance that I needed a little time by myself). Since I like to walk, and I am antisocial when I do because I wear my Sony Walkman, my hostess directed me to the local parks, advised me of their safety, gave me a key to her house and turned me loose.

The children in the school were *more* than prepared for my visit. They were enthusiastic, with signs to welcome me. They had read my books, were buying my books (which had been ordered by the librarian well in advance so they would be there and available), and were prepared with lots of questions. Parents had been invited to come to the school when I was there — and they did. A local newspaper reporter and photographer came. The principal attended two of the three sessions I did with the kids. (This is a very telling thing, I think — the interest and enthusiasm of a principal makes an enormous difference.)

The kids gave me a gift which they had chosen with great care and attention to my interests. (They knew from some promotional material that I collect patchwork quilts, so they gave me a lovely book about patchwork quilts.) Certainly, I don't expect or need a gift from kids, but it is charming and thoughtful evidence of their interest and affection.

I was paid my honorarium before I left. I was taken to the airport, of course, and I came back to Boston feeling very pleased about a fruitful and enjoyable trip.

— Lois Lowry, author of
  FIND A STRANGER,
  SAY GOOD-BYE

A Good Visit — What Makes It?

A good visit to a school begins with an early invitation, stating the honorarium they can offer and what use they would like to make of my time. I respond with suggestions and ideas and outline what they can expect from me.

The most important thing is for the students and staff to prepare by reading some of my books. The cliché, "The more you put into it, the more you get out of it," definitely works here. I am repeatedly told that there are few things that create interest and excitement in reading as the upcoming visit of an author. The students love it, too, when their teachers, principals and other administrators are also reading the books. This establishes a rapport and a camaraderie that utilizes my visit as a catalyst.

Then, if the schedule is worked out so that I have enough time with each group, and if arrangements have been made ahead to handle the requests for autographs, the visit does what it should do — for me and the students and everyone else involved, it satisfies and invigorates.

— Doris Buchanan Smith, author of
  A TASTE OF BLACKBERRIES

2

SET THE TRAP, LOAD THE BAIT

How To Seek Out and Capture Live Authors

Because of our mutual interest in encouraging students to read and to create original stories, teachers, librarians, parents and authors are natural allies. So in recent years, it is not surprising that all of us have joined together to provide students with author-related programs. We know that by giving young people opportunities to meet the writers and illustrators of the books they like, we encourage them to improve their reading and writing skills and to pursue the joy of reading even more.

Despite popular belief, all authors are not dead or living in the south of France. Many are very alive and well. They dwell in any and all of our fifty states — from New York to Oregon, from Georgia to California, from Texas to Alaska, from Missouri to Hawaii. And unless you and your students are intrigued with the macabre, most live authors are more fun than dead ones, and they are much easier to reach by telephone or via the postal service.

Authors and illustrators can be found speaking to student and teacher groups nationwide. For scheduling days in schools, hundreds of creative people are readily available upon request.

The Truth About Authors

Authors are often the most extraordinary, ordinary people in the world. Since they don't wear uniforms or have distinguishing marks, we may pass them on the streets or in shopping centers without noticing them.

I know of no other celebrities who can be so public and still retain their privacy. Most authors can slip into and out of the public spotlight and in between public engagements can lead as normal lives as they choose.

I think it is wonderful and important for students to become aware that exceptionally talented and gifted people are human beings who are actually not so very different from teachers, students and parents.

— Arnold Adoff, author of
BLACK IS BROWN IS TAN

— Chris Van Allsburg,
author and illustrator of
JUMANJI

Smooth As Silk

There's a festival every other year in Downer's Grove, Illinois, where a tremendous amount of planning takes place. Authors and artists are signed up well in advance and the children read a great many books while working up to the festival. Before the event, the speakers are sent packets of information and even marked maps.

The authors and artists go there for one day, visiting various schools. Each school is decorated with all sorts of book-related items and the children are primed to ask questions. The author is made to feel like someone really important.

Then on Saturday, there's a giant book fair, where the kids buy books in one room and go to another where the authors and artists are seated at tables, ready to autograph. They have "runners" to fetch coffee and everything is done to make the guests comfortable. It ends with a luncheon. Besides all this, the writers and artists are given an honorarium.

— Stella Pevsner, author of
I'LL ALWAYS REMEMBER YOU,
MAYBE

Special Note About Illustrators

As you select **authors** to speak to students, don't neglect to include **illustrators** in your considerations.

Most book illustrators have as thorough knowledge of plot development and structure of a good story as do most professional writers. In order to prepare proper illustrations, an artist must understand character motivation and the mood created by the text. And to the great enjoyment of students and teachers, presentations by illustrators tend to be more visual because they often feature prints and/or slides.

So, within these pages, every time we say **"author,"** keep in mind that the word **"illustrator"** may be interchangeable.

Selecting Your Author

**What are the best methods
for selecting an author (or illustrator)?**

First, find out whose books are of major interest to your students and teachers.

**Is it important to pick an author
whom the students like?**

Absolutely. Choosing authors whom students enjoy and respect is extremely important to the success of a program. The more students appreciate an author's works, the better they will respond to their visitor.

Should teachers agree with the choice?

By all means. Teachers should appreciate the author's works too. After all, teachers are the ones who will present much of the information about the author and initiate class involvement in the author's books. Enthusiasm in teachers builds enthusiasm in students. If teachers are not pleased with the choice of author, that enthusiasm can be diminished.

**Should we select authors whose books
are intended for the participating grade levels?**

Yes, with certain qualifications. It is certainly of benefit if most of the students can read the author's books. **However**, and I think this is a **big HOWEVER** and one which you should consider most carefully: Because of the restricted time in preparation for the author's visit, by reading some of the author's books to their classes, teachers have the opportunity to introduce higher level materials. Since the "hearing" vocabularies of most students are much higher than their "reading" vocabularies, an author can be selected whose works are one or two years above the grade level of the chosen classes.

**Should we select an author
who writes thought-provoking books?**

I've been asked this question many times so I am cautious in my answer. I'm always afraid the questioner is asking if the books should be serious in intent — such as ones which involve an in-depth study of some kind or teach a lesson or a moral.

In the past, it was considered that a quality juvenile book had to either propose a moral or teach how to build a clubhouse, campaign for public office, or some such thing. No matter how attractive were the bookjackets, or how exciting were their titles, or how many times we said these were really enjoyable books, students realized they were being handed additional textbooks to study.

However, in recent years, children's books are not so obviously didactic. Most thoughtful writers offer valuable insights into the interactions of characters and are bold enough to pose questions without always concluding with simplified or obvious answers.

Serious books don't have to be realistic or tragic to affect our thinking — they can be wildly humorous and highly entertaining. Jean Merrill, author of the very funny book, THE PUSHCART WAR, and I were discussing Robert Cormier's THE CHOCOLATE WAR, and Jean said: "Bob and I write about the same things, but he approaches the subjects with grave concern and I approach them with humor."

Most writers of good books, whether they deal with the joys or sorrows of life, offer insights into human nature and examine thinking processes. Their books provide valuable platforms for classroom discussions. They can also entertain. These are the types of books you want students to read. These are the authors you should attempt to capture.

Should we review the author's books before inviting him or her?

You certainly should. Although it's difficult for me to believe, I have been contacted by teachers and librarians who have never read one of my books, yet they ask me to speak at a school or dinner. That is really buying a pig in a poke!

What if we really admire the works of an author, but some of the language or the subject matter may be questionable for presentation in schools?

I don't believe in censorship, but I firmly believe in one's right to select. You should choose an author whose works express philosophies you consider beneficial to the intellectual and emotional growth of your students.

Most authors of juvenile books use words selectively and prudently. Editors also show considerable caution. If the language used is strong or crude, they have concluded such words are necessary to the content of the story. Authors and editors know they must be willing to stand by their decisions and withstand resulting criticism.

But what if a teacher feels uncomfortable with certain words or sections in a book?

I don't think any teacher should present materials to a class if these materials make him or her feel uncomfortable.

But if teachers haven't read a book before reading it aloud to the class, what can they do when they encounter some foul language?

Anyone who is naive enough to attempt to read **anything** aloud to an audience, without first having reviewed the materials, shouldn't be teaching. Even professional actors, who have all the skills of voice control and

My Darkest Days

Now for some horror stories. There have been times when I wasn't paid. Other times I have been asked to buy my own plane tickets and pay my hotel bills, then have had to wait months for reimbursement and call and ask for payment to boot. (I no longer make any trips without prepaid tickets.)

But the one I remember with the most misery occurred very close to home. I have no compunction about naming the school — the Martin Luther King School in Cambridge, Massachusetts, a public elementary school. The Cambridge Public Library had sponsored the event and paid authors to come. Each author was assigned to a school.

Unknown to me, prior to my visit, the school principal, having been advised of my impending visit, had leafed through one of my books. He saw a "swear word" — a word that offended him. He did not, of course, read the entire page, or chapter, or book — only that one word. He decided my books were unsuitable and called for their removal from the hands of the students. He did not cancel my visit — nor did I know this had happened.

On the appointed day, I went to the school. No one greeted me. I went to the library, and the librarian consulted a schedule and told me what classes I was to go to and the times. On my own, I found those classrooms.

In one classroom, the teacher greeted me at the door and told me that he felt my books were too mature for his students — a fifth grade — so he had not acquainted them with anything I had written. He then turned the class over to me for an hour, and he sat in the back of the room, correcting papers, while I attempted to use the time to explain who I was to thirty kids

(continued)

(continued)

who had never heard of me. I asked, "Has anyone read any of my books?"

One girl raised her hand and said, "I read part of one."

Later I discovered that the principal had taken the book from her when she was partway through.

In another class, I began (as a way of telling unprepared students about myself and why I was there) to read a passage from one of my books. The teacher, a gray-haired woman, interrupted me to say, "Please don't read from your books."

The whole day was a nightmare. Apparently, from what I was able to piece together afterward, the teachers had been advised by the principal that I wrote disgusting and unsavory books, but that there was no way he could prevent my visit because the public library had arranged it.

I did get paid. But that wasn't the important thing. I wasted a day and I was humiliated in a way that I didn't deserve. More importantly, the kids got absolutely nothing from my visit.

In the class where the teacher told me not to read from my books, she went on to say, "Tell them how important it is to write complete sentences."

Well, that's not my job. Maybe it's hers. Nor was it my job to baby-sit for the teacher who sat in the back of the class, smirking, while I tried to control thirty bored and unruly kids.

— Lois Lowry, author of
  A SUMMER TO DIE

I'll Never Forget...

My horrifying discovery that a woman who said, "That was interesting. I should try reading a child's book," was the librarian.

— Mary Francis Shura, author of
  MISTER WOLF AND ME

emphasis of words at their command, know better than to present material "cold."

But don't some teachers like to "live the story for the first time" with their students?

These teachers deserve to be shocked and caught with the writer's words in their mouths. There is simply no excuse for such lack of professional preparation, except unabashed naiveté or laziness.

But when reading a book aloud, isn't it all right if teachers omit sections or change a few words?

When a teacher changes words or deletes sections, by the end of the next recess, every student in the class will know what words were changed or what parts were omitted. When those words are read out of context, their use is often blown out of proportion.

But what if we haven't read all of the author's books before inviting him or her?

No one says you have to use **all** of the author's books in your program, but beforehand, you most certainly should select and review those you plan to share with the classes.

In selecting an author, you should seek out the type of materials that you feel are important and suitable to present and discuss with students of specific age groups. You want materials that will benefit and expand processes of thinking and encourage discussion. And appropriate materials are, oh, so easy to find. There are so many good writers today who explore the human condition with insight and humor, with realism and imagination. All you have to do is read their books and you will find your options are enormous in number and versatility.

So explore, review, then select.

The Biggest and the Best

Should we invite the most prominent authors?

It makes little difference whether or not an author's book has made the bestseller list. Invite the author who most intrigues your students.

Aren't the most prominent authors usually the busiest?

Sometimes. But the authors your students and teachers may find most interesting may not be the ones who are currently the "hottest" on the national scene. It's not uncommon for a book to become very popular in Illinois, but go unnoticed by people in Georgia or New York. This can also happen from city to city.

How does this occur?

In one community a librarian or teacher discovers a wonderful book and starts indicating his or her enthusiasm. Other librarians become interested and order copies, and teachers begin suggesting the book to their students. Sometimes students find a book and start a chain-of-reader movement among their friends and classmates. So a book that is barely noticed in other areas of the country may become extremely popular in your particular city or state.

How can we be sure the author we select will be able to come to our school?

You can't. So I suggest you begin with three to five authors in mind.

Before inviting a prospective author, should we check with others who have used him or her?

Of course! It's a proper and advantageous screening process. Investigate and ask for recommendations. You want to be certain the author you invite is able to relate well to your students and teachers.

Is it wiser to invite authors who have won awards?

Not necessarily. Book awards are presented on the basis of achievements in writing, not on the author's ability to speak. Some winners of awards are not the best speakers.

All authors who write **for** children do not feel comfortable in speaking **to** children. Some authors of juvenile books prefer to speak to adults about the formats, approaches and trends in children's book development, and they will simply refuse to speak to children's groups.

Isn't that strange?

Not particularly. An author's preference for a certain audience isn't any stranger than the choices of teachers who feel more comfortable teaching college classes rather than junior high school students or kindergartners. The preference is determined by knowing one's own personality and range of skills. It doesn't necessarily mean they don't like children. The choice depends more on one's processes of thinking and approaches to teaching and speaking.

During early program planning stages, ask the author which age groups he or she prefers. Don't try to mix and match. If you want a successful program, select the right author for the proper age group.

Plan Ahead When Scheduling Authors

How far ahead of the event should we contact an author?

Six months to one year. Some authors schedule two years in advance.

How can we contact an author?

1. Consult the author's books to find out what companies publish his or her works. Then:

   a. Write a letter to the author, expressing what type of program you have in mind and the age range of your students. Invite the author to speak and ask how much the fee might be. Mail your letter to the author, in care of the publisher, making sure you enclose a stamped envelope so all the publisher has to do is fill in the author's address and forward it; or

   b. Write a letter to the publisher and make the necessary inquiries. In order to direct your letter to a particular person in the company, refer to WRITER'S MARKET, Bowker's BOOKS IN PRINT, or LITERARY MARKET PLACE to obtain the name of the senior editor of the juvenile division or the young adult division, whichever is appropriate. Within a matter of days, the

Unrewarding!

It seems to me that writers are sometimes asked to talk with children who are too young or too old. This can be difficult for the writer and boring for the children.

— Clyde Robert Bulla, author of CONQUISTA

I book engagements at least one year in advance. Some teachers or principals call to ask if I'm available ''next month'' and seem surprised when I say, ''I'm not sure I'm available next year.''

— Theodore Taylor, author of THE MALDONADO MIRACLE

— Madeleine L'Engle, author of
A WRINKLE IN TIME

Time Is Valuable

You should understand that the author is a *business* person and that time spent away from the desk is valuable time that must be paid for. Too many authors are still speaking for "honor and glory" instead of money.

— Dorothy Francis, author of
CAPTAIN MORGANA MASON

Corbett's Law

Don't talk for free. People tend to be too casual about things they get for nothing, including speakers.

— Scott Corbett, author of
THE HOMERUN TRICK

Let's Make a Deal

Once, when someone was harassing me to come to a school because a certain teacher almost demanded it, I said, "Swell. Do you think the teacher would agree to a trade-off? Will she spend a Saturday typing my manuscript?" My offer was not well received.

— Stella Pevsner, author of
I'LL ALWAYS REMEMBER YOU,
MAYBE

editor will either respond to you directly or pass on your inquiry to the author; or

2. You may know of a group that has had your choice of author as a speaker. Upon contacting a member of that group, you may be given the address and even the telephone number of the author. Now you have a choice of writing a letter or phoning the author directly.

Would most authors rather be contacted via their publisher?

It varies from author to author.

Some insist that arrangements be made through their publishers, because they would rather not discuss fees or personally take the time to schedule engagements. In some cases, when an author's services are in great demand and his or her time commitments are staggering, the author may wish to rely on the publisher's selectivity. And some authors even think it's good business to keep their publishers aware of the number of personal appearance invitations.

Other authors insist upon making their own commitments, because they have found it is better to discuss the arrangements firsthand in order to avoid misunderstandings.

How can we know which way the author prefers?

You can't. So try either method of contacting the author and, in response, you will be told how the arrangements should be made.

A Fair Price

How much should we expect to pay an author per day?

The amount varies from author to author.

When I sent questionnaires to a number of authors, I was hoping to be able to arrive at an average figure, but most of them declined to list a set price and wrote instead, "My fee varies." Those who did fill in an amount indicated that fees "begin at $300.00 per day, plus expenses," and one author responded: "My standard fee is $2,000.00 per day, plus expenses for travel, meals and lodging."

Be that as it may, $300.00 per day, plus expenses, is a bargain — anything less is perhaps a "steal." When scheduling an author to speak at a convention or to conduct a complete workshop, you will probably have to pay more.

But can't authors speak for less?

It is virtually impossible for an author to visit a school for less, unless he or she places little or no value on the expenditure of time.

Contrary to rumors, most authors are not fabulously wealthy, especially writers of juvenile books. An author of an adult book stands the chance of making four and five times more from book sales. Of course, there are exceptions, but these are indeed exceptions. Very few become top money-makers from literary endeavors.

The creative person, whether he or she is a writer or an artist, must by necessity find means to subsidize the time spent on new works. A writer may spend months and months on a new book, receiving little or no advance from the publisher.

I recently spoke with a very well-known writer of children's books who told me she had spent two years working on what she thought was her best book. However, when she sent the completed manuscript to the publisher, the editor wanted her to make many revisions, which would require another two or three months of work. Although she wanted to try, she was afraid that she **could not afford to finish the book**. Making the necessary revisions would postpone the book's publication date for another year. With no royalties coming in, the author's income would be seriously affected. To make matters worse, her oldest child needed braces on his teeth, a loan was due at the bank, and the family car had just died.

There are times when writers simply can't afford to begin new books. They have to work at full-time jobs and do their writing at night and on weekends. Many must further supplement income by scheduling speaking engagements. This situation isn't new. We might recall that in order to avoid bankruptcy, Mark Twain went on a worldwide speaking tour. Charles Dickens subsidized his income by making personal appearances. So did Laura Ingalls Wilder.

One must also consider that an author's one-day visit to a school does not constitute one day's work. If the author is conscientious, he or she may spend several days in preparation for the event. Time spent traveling long distances to and from schools must also be considered, as well as the loss of part of another day in readjusting to a work schedule after returning home. All together, time for preparation, travel, and readjustment for a one-day visit to a school probably involves at least three days of the author's time — often more.

But don't authors owe something to their readers and the community?

Yes, they do, and the majority of writers feel such responsibility. But first and foremost, authors believe their prime responsibility is to provide their readers with **good books**, and most of them work very hard to accomplish that. Many fulfill responsibilities in their own community by making presentations to local schools and organizations for lower fees, and a number are given free of charge.

By the same token, it is also fair to ask if communities should take some responsibility in sponsoring the work of creative people. The answer is rather obvious. If a community wants to produce more creative people, it certainly should lend support. Had a local school paid Vincent van Gogh to speak to classes, perhaps he wouldn't have had to write so many desperate letters to his brother Theo, begging for money, and he might have died with both ears intact.

The Local Express

Wouldn't it be cheaper to invite a local author?

Yes, it would, but the price of the fee offered should not be less. The money you save should **only** be on expenses for travel, meals and lodging. But regardless of the quality of their writing or their ability to relate to an audience, for some strange reason, too many people feel out-of-town

Authors Have To Eat Too!

How I wish I could visit schools and libraries "free of charge," but bills have to be paid; a day lost from the typewriter is a day that cannot be replaced. As salaried teachers, librarians, principals, superintendents, etc., I hope you will understand this situation. Writers must earn money in order to eat, pay taxes, and have a domicile and office, unless, of course, they're subsidized. I'm not that lucky.

— Theodore Taylor, author of
  THE MALDONADO MIRACLE

Proper Fees Assure Commitments

I have no idea what others charge, but my fee is $500.00 for one day; several days are $400.00 each, minimum; $1,000.00 to be *sure* I come; and $2,000.00 to be sure I cancel any other engagement.

— Garth Williams, illustrator of
  Laura Ingalls Wilder's
  LITTLE HOUSE books

Money Talk

It would be appreciated if the question of the fee was decided before writing to the writer, leaving it up to him or her to thus make a decision about refusing or accepting. Asking the writer what he or she charges is embarrassing and, I believe, unfair.

— Julia Cunningham, author of
  THE TREASURE IS THE ROSE

Most Authors Can't Afford the Luxury of Speaking Just for Pleasure

Some beginning writers may wish to speak for the practice, or the publicity, or because they have the time and therefore the luxury of speaking just for the pleasure. But busy, professional authors lose precious writing time (both the travel and presenting days), and though they may enjoy the travel, the speaking and the audience tremendously, they need reimbursement to facilitate it.

— Berniece Rabe, author of
  NAOMI

authors are worth every penny they are paid, but local authors shouldn't be paid as much. I've never understood this because local authors have the same needs as out-of-towners to buy groceries, and they also have to make house payments.

Since we don't have to pay travel expenses, wouldn't it be cheaper to start a new program with a local author?

Cheaper? Yes. Better? Not necessarily. It depends on what kind of an event you decide you should have and how much attention you wish to generate.

Bring an author from New York or California and you can be almost assured of attaining coverage in the local media. No matter how competent local authors may be, rarely are they given as much attention from local television, radio and newspapers. As one author told me: "The only time I make the news in my hometown is when I *don't* speak to local groups."

For Services Rendered

Once we contact the publisher or the author, should we simply ask about the expected fee, or is it permissible to discuss price?

Whether or not the writer is a creative genius of the first magnitude, you are in the process of making a business contract. Business arrangements should always be open to discussion.

If interest is expressed in coming to your school, but the editor or author quotes a fee that you cannot possibly meet, you have every right to say so, then mention a figure you can afford. The editor or author may very well accept your price or offer a compromising figure.

Don't be tempted to guess the reasons why editors or authors have agreed to a lower fee. It doesn't mean that the author is down-and-out and selling apples on the street corner or that the author intentionally quoted a higher price to gain a bargaining position. Sometimes authors accept engagements at lower-than-usual prices because a specific type of program intrigues them, or they wish to strengthen their following in a particular geographical area, or they would simply like to get away from the typewriter for a few days.

Is it permissible to try to convince an author to accept a lower fee?

It is permissible, but tacky. I think it's enough to ask for a price and offer an alternative. Personally, I would feel uncomfortable in haggling over money with The Brothers Grimm or Hans Christian Andersen, or even with contemporary writers and illustrators, such as Lois Lowry and Garth Williams.

The Role of Publishers

Don't publishers sometimes pay a portion of the author's expenses?

Rarely. Unless the publisher is engaging the author for a publicity tour or the occasion you are planning provides unusual exposure for the author's books, publishers usually will not pick up the tab or even offer assistance.

Don't you think they should?

No. Publishers are in the business of publishing books, not of providing the services of speakers.

Checklist for Scheduling an Author

- ☐ Contact the author at least six months to one year in advance. If you don't, the author may already be booked.

- ☐ Be absolutely sure there is a thorough understanding of the amount of the author's fee and who will pay for travel, meals and lodging expenses. Unless otherwise specified, the author's fee **does not** include expenses, all of which you must provide.

- ☐ Determine if the author or the publisher prefers to make travel and lodging arrangements or if you are to do so.

- ☐ Be absolutely sure you and the author agree on the number of times the author is expected to speak, the length of each session, the size of audiences, and the ages of the students who will be participating.

- ☐ After all details are agreed upon, to avoid any misunderstandings, write a letter to the author recapping your agreement.

- ☐ When arrangements are concluded and confirmed, immediately ask the author or publisher to send a copy of the author's biography and bibliography.

Utilizing Both Out-of-Towners and Local Authors at the Same Event.

In developing multiauthor events, such as Young Authors' Days and Children's Literature Festivals, unless you have money to burn, it is doubtful that you can afford to bring all the authors from other cities and states. So you must also invite local authors to conduct sessions.

The Children's Literature Festival at Central Missouri State University invites about a dozen out-of-state authors each year, but the other twelve live less than one hundred miles away. These local authors comprise a core of support, because they return year after year to make presentations. I am always pleased at the generosity and graciousness of the local authors. Knowing the out-of-towners will receive most of the publicity and attention, the local authors are content to play second fiddle because they are so supportive of the program. You understand, many of these local authors are considered top-notch writers in their own right and are often the featured headliners at other events.

If you are developing multiauthor programs, the establishment of a group of local speakers is probably a necessity. However, you must make sure their generosity is not abused. Too often, local writers are the first

Travel Time Must Be Considered

For local presentations (up to 100 miles round-trip from Laguna Beach), I charge $150.00 per day.

For greater distances that require overnight stay, I charge $250.00 a day, plus travel expenses of .20 per mile, motel and meals. If air transportation is used rather than surface, I charge the cost of an economy-class ticket, plus transportation to and from home and the airport.

If this daily rate seems high, I must point out that I lose a day of work on each travel day. So if the presentations are to last three days, I'm actually involved in a five-day venture because of travel.

— Theodore Taylor, author of
THE MALDONADO MIRACLE

— William MacKellar, author of
THE WITCH OF GLEN GOWRIE

— Gerald McDermott,
adapter and illustrator of
ARROW TO THE SUN

Everyone Benefits!

I visited a small school in Oxford, Pennsylvania, where there was total school participation in the one-day visit, with two assembly presentations and ample opportunity for students to come to the library and meet the author. There was a good librarian, strong teacher support, and community and school board involvement and presence. I also visited a larger school in suburban Pittsburgh where all these same good things happened, including use of my books to enrich curriculum units. And I always recommend a visit to the Greenville, South Carolina, Middle School where the librarian, Pat Scales, has made reading the in-thing to do — for students and their parents.

In all these cases, arrangements and schedules were clear and precise, preparation by teachers and students was outstanding, and the author was treated as an honored guest. Everyone benefited!

— Barbara Robinson, author of
THE BEST CHRISTMAS
PAGEANT EVER

to arrive and the last to be paid for their services. It is not an enjoyable experience to be taken for granted. Do not allow this to happen at your events. Take special care that **all** speakers are properly welcomed, courteously attended during the course of the day and the evening, promptly paid, and individually thanked for their efforts.

No Two Authors Are Alike

You may have begun to suspect that arrangements made with authors must be made on an individual basis. That is true. Of the authors and illustrators I've met, all have one thing in common — each is very different from the other in style and personality. No matter how you arrange your program, you will find that the flavor of the author's personality and his or her individual approach to audiences will affect the overall. For better or worse, the author is that added ingredient which seasons and adds the finishing touch to the success of your planned event.

In later chapters, we will discuss the importance of proper planning and scheduling your event in order to best utilize the skills and talents of your guest author. But for now, we must start adding some figures — the author's fee and the expenses for travel, meals and lodging. Soon you will have a total of costs. Then you must find the funds to make your dream a reality. That may be easier than you think.

Sandy Asher

3

$ $ DOLLARS AND SENSE $ $

Methods for Financing and Supporting Your Programs

After you have contacted your author and have arrived at an approximate cost for your program, the time has come for your committee to sit down with your school principal to present your plan.

If your principal likes the idea, but says there aren't enough funds in the school budget to finance such a program, ask how much the school can afford.

Whatever is offered by the principal, even if that amount is no more than one hundred dollars, accept the offer and assure him or her that you are confident your committee can raise the remainder.

If your principal agrees, present the plan to the president of your PTA or PTO. Many times programs are fully or partially financed by these organizations. If yours won't or can't, you must look elsewhere.

Many states have councils for the arts which offer financial support for author-related programs. If such groups are established in your area, contact them. Some councils are easy to approach and prompt to respond. Others will bury you and your idea under bureaucratic red tape and mountains of forms which must be filled out in triplicate, leaving you to conclude that your time would be better spent elsewhere.

Placing PIE Into Action

There is a new acronym, PIE, which stands for PARTNERS IN EDUCATION. This increasingly popular movement encourages businesses in a community to take an active part in supporting educational projects for students. With your proposed program, you have the opportunity to place PIE in action.

Have your committee list all prospective companies in your community. Don't forget fast-food chains because many franchisers urge their managers to build community goodwill by taking an active part in civic and philanthropic projects.

— Patricia Reilly Giff, author of the CASEY VALENTINE series

Creating Harmony of Warmth and Interest

A gold star goes to the schools of Waynesville, Missouri! These schools are an example of how to create a warm and caring reception for a visiting author. As a result, I was put completely at ease, and in a relaxed fashion, I was able to give my very best. The children sensed and responded to this harmony — rapport was splendid and they behaved their very best. They listened carefully and, as hoped for, took renewed interest in reading, which was what it was all about in the first place.

— Ida Chittum, author of
TALES OF TERROR

— Thomas Rockwell, author of
HOW TO EAT FRIED WORMS

If one goes about it in the right way, financing is easy to raise. After all, you are not asking for money for yourselves. You are asking people to sponsor a project to encourage children to read and write. Most people will recognize the merit of your cause and rise to the occasion by assisting financially.

Many community service organizations are also geared to sponsor beneficial projects — Optimist clubs, women's leagues, the Kiwanis, the Chamber of Commerce, and others are excellent sources for financial aid.

The System That Never Fails

I was told by one school librarian about a system for raising funds that never fails. "If three women go into a businessman's office and ask for support for a worthy cause for children, they always come away with a check or cash in hand," she advised with a knowing smile.

Give it a try.

Show Your Appreciation

Once you have found local sponsors, don't forget them. It is infinitely easier to keep a sponsor than it is to find new ones. So be sure to pave all your steps with goodwill and cultivate the continuing support of sponsors, by:

- Listing their names on any and all printed materials.

- Sending invitations to them to attend the functions and to meet the author.

- Sending thank-you notes to them. Even have students and teachers who benefited from the sponsor's generosity send letters of appreciation.

- Taking photographs while the author is visiting, then sending copies to them.

- Sending a brief, but complete, report at the conclusion of your program on how the money was spent and what benefits were enjoyed by the children and teachers.

When schools pay proper respect to their sponsors, their benefactors will be eager to help again. One teacher told me, after sending a thank-you note and a report to a sponsor, she received another check for twice the amount. An enclosed note read: "This amount is next year's contribution. KEEP UP THE GOOD WORK!"

Now's Your Chance To Make People Feel Good!

When people in your community contribute to improving the lives of students and teachers, it makes them feel good. Now is your opportunity to give the business people and members of service groups in your community the opportunity to feel good. It's an enjoyable and most rewarding experience for your community, your students, your teachers, your committee and you.

Together, you are setting the stage for a wonderful, rewarding time to be had by all!

Another Important Source of Income — Sales of the Author's Books

For raising money, you have yet another ace in the hole. If you order copies of the visiting author's books directly from the publisher or a jobber, you can often purchase them at a thirty- to forty-percent discount. Since copies will be sent to you on consignment, you will only have to pay for the ones you sell and can return the remaining books. Sales from books can add a substantial sum to your coffers. One of my publishers told me that schools average selling $600.00 worth of books on visiting author days, which means a school can clear a profit of $180.00 to $200.00.

Several years ago, I was contacted to speak to all the classes, from second grade through junior high school, in Newton, Kansas. I presented four programs each day for ten days. By having bake sales and selling pecans, the local council of the International Reading Association had raised the finances to cover the two weeks. However, much to their surprise, the profits from books sold paid for all but two of my days. Therefore, they had enough money left over to sponsor another author program later that year.

**Should we sell books
during the author's visit?**

Yes! Many students, parents and teachers will want personally autographed copies, so you are not only selling books — you are providing a service.

**Do authors insist upon having their books
available for sale during speaking engagements?**

Of all the authors and illustrators who answered the questionnaires and returned them to me, not one said he or she insisted on books being sold during visits. However, I personally know two (who did not fill out the questionnaires) who definitely will not accept engagements unless their books are available for purchase.

**But what if our school has a rule
barring the sale of merchandise to students?**

Some schools have such a rule. If yours does, it does. But maybe it's time to consider changing the rule. Most schools have vending machines to dispense supplies and snacks. And they sell tickets for sports events and food at concession stands. Why not books? I would much rather see schools sell books than hot dogs and Cokes.

**If we offer books for sale,
might some parents complain?**

Let's face it — somewhere out there among the populace, there are a few parents who will complain about anything. Right? Right. But I can honestly say, in the hundreds of schools I have visited where books have been sold, I have never heard of such complaints. By sheer numbers

— Marian T. Place, author of
THE BOY WHO SAW BIGFOOT

Where Are the Books?

The main thing is to have books available for the students to buy. It is very discouraging to arrive at a school where no one has read your books and none are around for sale.

— Jan Greenberg, author of
NO DRAGONS TO SLAY

Give Students Time To See and Appreciate

I think children should not be hurried and made to stand in line when they want to look at books or illustrations. Their contact with normal, friendly writers and illustrators gives them the feeling that "we" are not extraordinary, and that they, too, may become writers if they have talent and work at it.

— Wilma Pitchford Hays, author of
YELLOW FUR
AND LITTLE HAWK

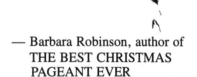

— Barbara Robinson, author of
THE BEST CHRISTMAS
PAGEANT EVER

Preparation and Book Sales Provide Program Success

Mary Ellen Russell, librarian at Rolla Middle School, does an exceptionally good job. She tries very hard to see that the children are familiar with the author's work and prepared with questions. They are also warned that only the author's books and bound autograph books will be signed, *not* scraps of paper!

Two local bookstores set up shop in the library for two days prior to the visit, plus the day of the visit, selling the author's books, along with regular stock, and donating ten percent of their receipts to the school (which pays for the visit).

— Sandy Asher, author of
TEDDY TEABURY'S
FABULOUS FACT

alone, there must have been some, but they have never been serious enough to warrant being mentioned to me. In fact, in schools where books were **not** available for sale, I have heard a number of complaints from students, teachers and parents, who sometimes seem to blame **me** for not insisting that books are on hand.

A couple of years ago, one school librarian had ordered books from my publishers, but at the last minute, because the principal feared criticism, he told her not to place them on sale. I had been asked to speak at the school open house, and that evening the auditorium was filled with parents and students. During the question and answer period, one parent asked in rather annoyed tones why copies of my books were not available for purchase.

Gentleman that he was, the principal stood up quickly and explained: "To avoid any criticism, we decided not to sell books."

Then at the audience's insistence, the somewhat flustered principal hurriedly helped the librarian set up a table and open the boxes. They enjoyed a land-office business.

Doesn't it concern you that some children who want books cannot afford to buy them?

Yes. Not only does it bother me, it pains me. Although I try to put on blinders, I still see those students who obviously don't have enough money to buy a book.

On the other hand, I see students who, for the very first time in their lives, are motivated to buy a book of their very own, instead of purchasing the latest recording by Sting or Madonna. That one book may be the first step in acquiring a personal library. Or, at least, I like to think that it might.

If students aren't encouraged to buy books at school or by their parents, where will they get the idea? Television doesn't promote the sale of books. Television sells fast foods, sugar-coated cereals and hard rock, and it encourages viewers to watch more television. Too frequently parents aren't as interested in promoting reading as they should be. So if students are ever going to get "hooked" on books, schools must take the initiative and set the example.

You are offering students the opportunity to buy a book and have it autographed by its author. Why do we want personally autographed books? I don't know. Rarely does an autograph make the book more valuable for resale, but it does reveal that we have had, for even a short period of time, personal contact with its creator. Whether or not we ever show the book to anyone else, it is signed proof of our encounter. To varying degrees, we treasure both the book and that moment in some special way.

What is the best way to order books?

It depends upon what you wish to achieve in sales.

If your group wishes to make a profit (which may or may not be applied to the cost of the program), then order directly from the publisher. Depending on the quantities you order, you may receive up to a forty-percent discount. But you must keep in mind that that percentage is not pure profit since you will be billed for the cost of shipping, and you must also pay for the return shipment of unsold books.

Some school groups that don't wish to make a profit, still order books directly from publishers, estimate the shipping costs, then sell the books to students and teachers at cost.

Ordering directly from publishers does require some lead time. You should place your orders at least one month in advance of your program to insure the books arrive in time. To obtain a variety of the author's books, you may have to order from more than one publisher since many authors are published by two or more.

You should also be aware that since you probably do not have an open account with the publishers, some may send the books C.O.D., making it necessary for you to pay up-front money. Others will send you the books on consignment.

To save time and effort, some groups order books from local jobbers. The discounts are not as high, but the jobber can secure books from several publishers. Some jobbers will also pick up unsold books, which saves you extra shipping costs.

Keep in mind that you are responsible for the condition of the books returned. The publisher will not accept damaged merchandise.

One librarian told me she returns unsold books library rate because it's the cheapest way. And it probably is. However, you would be well advised to ship returns by methods which provide you with proof of shipment and insured merchandise.

In some communities, industrious bookstore managers specialize in setting up book fairs for schools or will set up sales in your school for a special function. They will take care of all ordering, shipping and sale of books. Some will even pay you a percentage of the profits.

Who is usually placed in charge of the ordering and sale of books?

Most often the librarian is "elected," but it's too much to expect one person to handle this task. An accurate count of money and books sold is essential at all times. Be sure to offer plenty of assistance and assistants.

When should books be made available for purchase?

Some groups start selling books a day or so before the author arrives, but more energetic groups make books available at least one week in advance, which undoubtedly increases sales.

How do we decide how many books should be ordered?

If you are selling books for the first time, your guess is as good as mine. Some groups order hundreds of books and sell out. Others order a few dozen and have leftovers. Except in extremes, the economic conditions of the community seem to have little effect on the number of sales. I have spoken in very affluent communities where only a small number of books are purchased and in blue-collar neighborhoods where books are bought by the stacks.

I think the purchase of books is dependent upon three factors:

1. How well the students like the books and the author.

2. How important the parents and educators feel it is to encourage students to take a personal interest in books.

3. How well the students and their parents have been informed about the availability of books.

Don't Forget the Teachers and Librarians

Many of my most appreciative listeners are teachers and librarians. More of them should be included in the group or possibly in a separate program (a tea or a lunch) where a writer can speak of her goals and hopes and plans in writing for children. It is easier for these educators then, to say: "Mrs. Hays told me, etc."

— Wilma Pitchford Hays, author of
   YELLOW FUR
   AND LITTLE HAWK

— Richard Peck, author of
   ARE YOU IN THE HOUSE ALONE?

A Fine Combination

The Tampa and Miami Book Fairs have always been very well organized. Everything goes like clockwork. The writers know exactly where to be and when. The children, brought in by bus from their schools, arrive right on schedule, full of questions. All the writers are taken out to lunch and dinner, with lots of good conversation thrown in.

— Mildred Lawrence, author of
GATEWAY TO THE SUN

Working Models

The Children's Literature Festival at Central Missouri State University, with Phil Sadler in charge, and the Tampa, Florida, Book Fair are very well organized and hospitable, and have good accommodations for guest speakers. A speaker feels among friends and can do his or her best in a relaxed manner.

This is also true of the Cape Cod "Writers in the Schools" program, which is well organized and has friendly reception.

— Wilma Pitchford Hays, author of
YELLOW FUR
AND LITTLE HAWK

While all three factors come into play, I think the major influence in number of sales is determined by how well the students and parents **are informed** and **reminded** that the author's books are available.

If you get the information to parents and students soon enough and complete enough, then more than likely you will sell a considerable number of books.

But if you wait until the last minute or fail altogether to let anyone know books are being sold, then be prepared to repack the cartons and pay the freight on the returns.

How should we notify parents that the author's books will be for sale?

If you want to encourage the sale of books, it is an absolute must that you send proper information to parents, telling them of the upcoming program featuring a visiting author and enclosing a list of titles and prices of available books. For example:

> Dear Parents:
>
> To encourage reading and creative writing in our students, on Wednesday, October 10, 1986, the renowned children's author, Eric Wordsworth, is invited to speak to the fifth- and sixth-grade classes.
>
> Because some students will want copies of Mr. Wordsworth's books for him to autograph, books can be purchased at school from October 3rd through October 10th. The books are being offered as a convenience for those who wish to purchase them.
>
> We plan for the following books to be available:
>
> ACROSS THE CREEK (hardcover) $6.95
>
> INTO THE MEADOW (softcover) $2.95
>
> THROUGH THE WOODS (hardcover) $7.95
>
> ABOVE THE CLOUDS (softcover) $2.35
>
> If you have any questions, please telephone us or send a note.
>
> Sincerely,
> Marian, the Librarian

To help avoid having a number of disappointed students who have forgotten to bring their money, send a reminder to parents the day before the author arrives.

Even after sending sufficient information and plenty of warning, on the day of the author's visit, you'll probably have parents rushing in at the last minute to bring forgotten checks or cash in response to urgent phone calls from anxious children.

Jumping All Hurdles

Although raising funds often requires considerable organization and effort, it is not an obstacle you can't overcome. In fact, many people thoroughly enjoy the challenge. An appropriate amount of work, coupled with perseverance and determination, will really pay off. Once finances are raised, you can begin concentrating on the other important aspects of developing your program.

Theodore Taylor

4

"SOMEHOW IT ALL COMES TOGETHER"

Important Planning Stages in Developing Successful Programs

Although I've had principals and teachers tell me, "Somehow it all comes together," I know better. In programs that are properly organized, nothing just happens by **somehow** or chance. Instead, **someone** or **some-ones** have expended time and effort to think and to place a workable plan into action.

If there's one thing my years of speaking in schools have taught me, it's that teachers and librarians have a genius for organizing a workable rank and file. They know how to arrange everything — from rescheduling the school day for special events to designating those persons who are to bring the cookies and punch.

In some cases, one or two people take charge and work out every detail. In other situations, responsibilities are allocated to several committee members. You know the personalities and capabilities of your colleagues. Organize and structure your program planning committee accordingly.

Bringing It All Together

To insure that your author-related program achieves the most success, the members of your committee must address themselves, to:

- Selecting the classes that will participate and making a schedule;

- Providing information and materials to prepare teachers and students to meet the author;

- Scheduling the author's time, travel, meals and lodging; and

- Giving attention to the one important step which is often ignored — planning ways to get the best media coverage.

While we will discuss these considerations individually in separate

— Betsy Byars, author of
THE SUMMER OF THE SWANS

chapters, you should be aware that your committee isn't allowed the luxury of dealing with them one at a time. More than likely you will be planning and implementing all aspects of your preparations simultaneously. So you had best begin making lists and checking them twice.

Getting the Most and the Best from Your Guest Author

Whether you are planning to host a Visiting Author Program, an Author-in-Residence Program, a Young Authors' Day, a Children's Literature Festival, or any variations on these four themes, be sure you schedule the activities to allow the author to function at his or her ultimate best.

In an attempt to allow more students to see the author, some program coordinators make the mistake of spreading the author's time too thin by scheduling too many sessions and making each one too short. While trying to beat the clock, it becomes impossible for the harried author to function at his or her very best. Because of the limited time, students are placed at a disadvantage too. They don't have enough time to ask questions, so they wind up feeling cheated.

Won't having the author speak to a school assembly offer more students the opportunity to see him or her?

Yes, but only from a far, impersonal distance. When an author must speak to a sea of faces, the speaker is limited in choice. Authors should not be expected to direct a presentation toward such wide and diverse age groups at one sitting. How would you like to try to teach a mathematics course to five grade levels in one session? That's why students are grouped by ages and developmental levels in school. Why should you expect an author to do what even the best teachers won't dare attempt? Authors are not elastic — they can be stretched only so far.

In today's society, students are accustomed to watching television and films. In these media, there are camera close-ups which allow the viewer to see the character's expression or reaction at near range. If students and teachers are going to meet an author, they will not feel satisfied unless they have the chance to experience that author, **close up** and in **full frame**.

Too many, too far, too much, and too little are not enough. The quality of the experience must not be sacrificed to accommodate quantity. Students and teachers expect and deserve to have the best possible personal contact with visiting authors.

How should we select which classes will participate?

In author-related programs, most schools select classes by grade levels. They arbitrarily decide that certain programs are best for the fifth grade or the sixth grade, others are more suitable for first and second graders, and so on. In higher grades, the classes are usually selected by subject matter, such as English or creative writing classes.

But what if we want all grades to participate in the program?

Fine — that is, if you have an author whose work and presentation is adaptable to all the grades in your school and if you have enough hours

Please! Check for Sound

I remember one junior high where I was ushered out into an open-air theater, with hundreds of hot, sweating students staring at me, only to discover that the P.A. system wasn't working. As I shouted out my talk, every joke and witticism fell flat. I filled out the allotted time with the dread feeling that I was facing a lynch mob.

— Paula Hendrich, author of SAVING AMERICA'S BIRDS

— Beverly Brodsky McDermott, author and illustrator of THE GOLEM

Adverse Conditions

A few places have had too many children in crowded places, with noisy outside interference, and a policy of "no touching" of the books. I *can* speak under these conditions, but not at my best because listeners are not at their best.

— Wilma Pitchford Hays, author of YELLOW FUR AND LITTLE HAWK of the author's time for him or her to meet with all the grades. And be absolutely sure **the author has agreed** to speak to all grades. Some authors refuse to speak to younger children; others will not speak to older ones. Most authors who create books in the juvenile and young adult fields write for specific age groups. Their books are not suitable for or adaptable to a wide range of grade levels.

Don't spring surprises! Don't pull an "Oh, by the way," or a "Now that you're here, we thought you'd be happy to know that we have been able to schedule time for you to speak to all the classes — grades one through twelve." It is only common courtesy to ask your author, **prior to arrival**, whether he or she is up to such a challenge.

But what if our sponsors want all the students to have an opportunity to meet the author?

That often happens, especially if the program is sponsored by the PTO, a state arts council, or even the school.

So the author can effectively meet with all classes you wish to include, it's much better to add days to the program than to squeeze everyone into shorter time frames. If your sponsors insist that all students participate, then clearly explain to them that they will need to provide more funds to extend the number of days or to pay for additional authors.

But won't the other students feel left out?

To prevent other students from feeling left out, one would hope that during the school year every grade has some special project or program.

Is it all right to take authors from room to room, just long enough to introduce them to other classes?

Don't do it! These Band-Aid visits are embarrassing to the author and unrewarding to students. The time spent with each class is far too short to be of value. It's like being invited to a birthday party and not being given any cake and ice cream.

One well-known author recently told me that ever so often a teacher or principal will take him by the arm and guide him from room to room, announcing: "Well, kids, here he is — a real live author!"

"I just want to hide," the author said, shaking his head. "I mean, what can one do? If I could dance, maybe I could perform a soft-shoe. I feel like I've been stuffed and placed on display. I really don't like it."

Dealer's Choice

When an author speaks to one or two grade levels, should every class in these grades have to participate?

Mandatory participation is a big mistake. As authors differ from each other, so do teachers. There are some teachers who feel that such programs are no more than added interruptions to their planned schedules and thoroughly resent being told their classes must be included. By the way, I am not implying that these are poor or lazy teachers. It may only mean they are more structured in their scheduling of curriculum. I assure you, there is nothing worse for a visiting author than to stand before a group and catch the cold stare of a teacher who obviously wishes the speaker

On the Spot!

The only thing that really sours me about a school visit is when I am scheduled for more sessions than the "up to four" I clearly agree to. Before I learn of these extra sessions, I am already embarked on the day. It really puts me on the spot. If I cancel the remaining sessions, I have no chance to explain to the students that it is not my fault and that it is *not* a misunderstanding. Whether I continue or refuse to continue, the students are the losers.

After one such grueling day — *nine* sessions instead of the stated four — I said, "If I had known how this was going to be, I would have sent a cardboard cutout and a tape recorder."

The thought-he-was-so-clever administrator laughed nervously and quipped, "We got more out of you than you expected, didn't we?"

"No," I said, "you got less."

The importance of what I have to share is not only my expertise and experience as a writer, but myself and my creative energy, bouncing some sparks off the students, as it were. If I am exhausted and parrot-tongued, there are no sparks left in me and the students do indeed receive less.

— Doris Buchanan Smith, author of A TASTE OF BLACKBERRIES

I Should Have Known Better

Because I've enjoyed all the places I've visited, I'm fortunate in not having a horror story to tell. Probably the most tiring experience for me, however, was a visit to a school where I had agreed beforehand to make more presentations than I should have, but I was geared up for it — and younger than I am now.

I was to meet with groups of children from the upper grades of the elementary school. The tiring part came when a very nice, but overly enthusiastic, PTA chairman told me that the younger children were excited about my visit from hearing the older kids discuss it. Therefore, she wondered if I would mind just "sticking my head in the door" of the primary and kindergarten rooms, and I agreed to do it.

The school was a big one with lots of doors in the early childhood wings, and Madam Chairman stuck my head in all of them. I'm not comfortable with just stepping into a room and having someone say, "Look at the author!" so on being introduced it seemed only friendly to ask the kids if they enjoyed books, then to chat with them briefly about my link with stories.

For teachers perhaps, or others who are accustomed to being on their feet and working with children all day, it would not have seemed tiring. But for those of us who face typewriters instead of people all day, although it's exciting to come face to face with our readers and flattering to be told that children would like to meet us, the sound of our own voices for too long a time can begin to get us down!

— Robert Burch, author of
    IDA EARLY COMES
    OVER THE MOUNTAIN

had stayed at home. Offer your teachers the choice of whether or not their classes participate.

But what if some teachers participate only because they don't want to be singled out as being uncooperative?

I wish they would **rather** be singled out, because sometimes their classes can be extremely disruptive to the day. The reluctant teacher's class is often poorly prepared, the students aren't as eager to ask questions, and their questions, when asked, are inferior to those posed by well-prepared students.

But don't you hate for their students to miss the experience of meeting an author?

Definitely. But I still prefer that participating classes are there by choice rather than by mandate.

Utilizing the Author's Time

How many sessions should we schedule for an author?

Never more than four sessions per day. However, some authors will not speak to more than two or three groups each day. So it is prudent to check with your author **before** scheduling the number of sessions.

What should be the maximum number of students per group?

I have found through experience that I can see as many as sixty, individual faces and am able to make direct contact with each student during a fifty-minute session. If you insist upon having more than sixty students in a group, you might as well schedule an auditorium-style program, crowd everyone together at one time, and forget about personal contact.

How long should each session last?

Unless the author is conducting a workshop in which students are actively engaged, fifty minutes (without a commercial break) is about as long as most students can tolerate sitting in one place. Some authors prefer forty minutes. Thirty minutes for primary grades is ample.

Time recommendations really vary and should depend on the skills and preferences of individual authors. Bear in mind that the author usually knows the best length of time required to give his or her most effective presentation. Be sure to check with each visiting author **beforehand** to determine what time allotments he or she desires.

What if we want to schedule fifty-minute sessions, but the author insists on a maximum of forty minutes?

Either adapt your schedule or find another author.

How much time between sessions should the author be allowed?

A minimum of fifteen minutes. Twenty minutes is even better.

Don't schedule other activities during break times, such as meeting the principal or school administrators, or being interviewed by members of the media. Authors really need time to regroup their thoughts and energies and, in most cases, to give their voices and smiles a chance to rest.

In junior high and high schools where time periods are not so flexible, authors may conduct sessions with only ten-minute breaks, but they should be allowed an open hour after two such sessions. Never schedule more than two sessions in a row.

Bring Out the Anchovies!

How much time should we allow for lunch?

At least one hour.

How should we plan meals for the guest author?

Very carefully and with some discussion with the author **before** plans are finalized.

The kinds of food and the amounts one might eat at home may be different from what a traveling speaker will eat during an engagement. And some people have special dietary needs and concerns, so also inquire about those your visiting author may have before planning menus.

As for breakfast, some authors prefer to eat alone; others like company. One author may like to breakfast at his hotel/motel before being picked up by the escort; others are satisfied to have donuts and coffee with teachers at school.

If you are taking the author to a restaurant for lunch, in order to allow plenty of time to eat without rushing, be sure you have reservations and that the service is prompt.

If you have planned for a small group to have lunch with the author, keep the group small — no more than eight persons.

For dinner, some authors may wish to eat alone; others are flexible and enjoy a planned gathering in a restaurant or a private home.

Do authors enjoy having meals in private homes?

I do. I find that teachers, librarians and their spouses are terrific chefs. I have eaten delicious meals in private homes and have collected a wide variety of recipes during my travels. However, some authors avoid having meals in private residences at all costs. So be sure to consult your author **before** concluding plans.

Whether dinner is arranged in a private home or a public gathering place, be sure there are enough tables, even if you have to set up card tables. I know of no one who likes to balance a plate on one knee and a glass on the other while meeting and talking with new acquaintances.

No matter how congenial or outgoing the author may be, you must consider that he or she has the added stress of meeting new people and adjusting to strange surroundings. Make your author as comfortable as possible at all times.

Should we plan lunch at school for the authors?

Some authors are agreeable to having lunch at the school. Others relax better if they leave the campus. But all authors appreciate enough time to eat lunch at leisure, without having to answer a thousand questions.

Personal Opinion

I really think 30 minutes per group is enough, even though periods run 45-50. Studies show people have no more than 20 minutes' attention span.

— Sandy Asher, author of
TEDDY TEABURY'S
FABULOUS FACT

— Brenda Wilkinson, author of
LUDELL

Bring on the Carbohydrates!

I tend to be a rebel in the group. I love to have lunch with the students. Yes, school cafeterias are noisy. Yes, the food is usually of high starch content. But I endure the noise and the carbohydrates for the pleasure of talking informally with the children. While eating with the students, I get capsulized, and sometimes highly imaginative, versions of information. I learn much about the community and the school. I find out which teachers are considered super great and which ones are, well — you know. Plus, I have always found that once the students realize the author is interested in their company, the visit becomes friendlier and the afternoon sessions go even better.

— David Melton, author of
WRITTEN & ILLUSTRATED BY...

Hard and Fast Rules for Survival

Avoid dinners in private homes. Wine and cheese parties, yes. Dinner, no!

I made this a hard and fast rule after one regrettable happening. After I had spent a long day speaking at several schools, my hostess insisted upon taking my husband and me to her home for dinner. Earlier that day we had driven several hundred miles to reach the city, so my husband and I were unusually tired and hungry.

Our hostess seated us on the patio and went inside the house to prepare dinner. After about 45 minutes, our hostess appeared and we were each served a half of a small, nearly raw chicken that was nested upon a few limp lettuce leaves. As I began to cut it up, I realized I couldn't eat. I sipped at the iced tea, which was warm and weak, and stirred sugar into it for nourishment — all the time, aware of my husband's frowning glances. We lost little time in excusing ourselves and going out to dinner on our own.

So my rules are:

Never dine in private homes. Never, never stay overnight in private homes. Insist on your own motel room.

There, you can relax and have time alone to go over your talks for the next day or days.

— Ida Chittum, author of TALES OF TERROR

Enjoys Staying in Homes

I don't hesitate to stay in the homes of acquaintances, and so far, I have never had an unpleasant experience. In fact, I have made close friends whom I might otherwise have missed cultivating.

By the way, anyone who turns down an invitation to stay at Virginia Boyd's home in Newton, Kansas, will miss the friendliest conversations and the best-cooked meals, including the greatest spiced cucumbers in the world!

— David Melton, author of WRITTEN & ILLUSTRATED BY...

Most authors are inquisitive and eager to learn more about the hosts and their community. Lunch often provides the author a chance to ask questions and become better acquainted.

Selecting Lodging for the Guest Author

While an elegant suite in the fanciest hotel may be grand, most authors don't expect or demand luxury. If the luxury hotel means additional miles of travel and inconvenience, most authors prefer a more modest, convenient location. However, they do appreciate a good, clean place to stay.

When you are making reservations for your author, take the time to check out the available hotel/motel accommodations well in advance. Be sure they are adequate and clean! If you plan far enough ahead, you can often select a specific room.

Do authors object to staying in private homes?

Some will flatly refuse. Either they feel uncomfortable staying in the homes of strangers or they need some time alone. Some will reluctantly acquiesce. Others will willingly agree.

But before booking any author in a private residence, you should **first ask** for the author's permission.

About Scheduling Evening Events

What if we would like to arrange a special function in the evening?

Especially when an author comes some distance, your group may want to have an open house or a special program at the school and invite parents and people in the community.

Do most authors charge more for evening engagements?

Some authors may include an evening speaking engagement in the price of their fee. Others expect to be paid extra. To conserve energy, some authors will insist that no afternoon sessions are scheduled if they are going to speak at an evening function. Others have high energy levels and are willing to work all day and into the night. However, never schedule an extra function without **first obtaining approval** from the author.

Words of Caution —

The mere act of scheduling an author to speak in the evening does not automatically assure that a large audience will assemble. You should know your community. In some towns and cities, parents are very responsive to school activities. In others, they avoid them like the plague.

There is nothing more disheartening for the author than to be introduced to an audience of two dozen people and three hundred empty chairs. If your community is not responsive to programs at school and you wish to have the the author speak to a group, select that group — such as the local council of the IRA, a writer's club or Friends of the Library.

Explore and Observe

When scheduling authors to speak at Young Authors' Days and Children's Literature Festivals, more coordination and effort is required because several authors are brought in. You may be involved with contacting as many as eight or more creative people. Because attending students may vary considerably in age — elementary, junior high and high school — most likely you will have to secure authors and illustrators whose works are compatible with the various age groups.

If you wish to plan a Young Authors' Day, the national or state council of the International Reading Association can inform you of other councils in your area that have ongoing Young Authors' Day activities and programs. You would be well advised to attend some of their functions. You will find the members of IRA councils to be most helpful in sharing their experiences with you and in offering good suggestions.

By the same token, if you are planning a Children's Literature Festival, it would be helpful to attend other festivals and observe.

The Unsung Heroes and Heroines

As you can plainly see, none of these events "somehow come together" without careful planning. The programs require much work and preparation.

Any sensible author realizes and appreciates the time and effort you have put forth. Although we authors receive most of the attention during these events, we are certainly aware that you teachers and librarians and your volunteer parents have spent hours in meetings and on the phone, missed lunches, and worked into many late nights and early mornings.

You are truly the unsung heroes and heroines of the successful author-related programs. It is you who bring the authors and the students together.

— Patricia Calvert, author of THE SNOWBIRD

A Most Successful Visit

I've had many pleasant experiences. I especially enjoyed a four-day stay in Texas, sponsored by combined school systems, visiting two schools per day and doing two programs at each. Books had been sold ahead of my visit, and time was allowed for autographing them in the library before and after the programs.

At noon, the librarian of the school where I had spent the morning would take me to a restaurant, where I would meet the librarian from the school I was to visit in the afternoon. Usually, the principals involved and the library coordinators of one or both systems also joined us for lunch. Afterward, I would go with the second librarian for the afternoon sessions. At the end of the school day, I was taken back to the hotel and allowed time to take a walk or a nap, or read the paper until time to meet a few of the librarians for dinner.

On one occasion, I was taken on a tour of the surrounding countryside, which I enjoyed immensely. During one of the evenings, there was a covered-dish dinner, in which almost all of the librarians participated, that was great fun. I was always returned to the hotel in time for a good night's sleep — but without time enough to risk "hotel-room-miseries" setting in!

Whenever I visit a school, in addition to meeting the school librarians of the area, I'm especially pleased if the children's librarians from the local public libraries have been invited to one of the programs or simply drop in for a chat. Likewise, the teachers of children's literature courses at colleges in the area are welcome. People who are interested in children and their books are a small enough group at best; it's good for us to get to know each other.

— Robert Burch, author of
  IDA EARLY COMES
  OVER THE MOUNTAIN

5

DOUBLE PLEASURE, TRIPLE FUN!

Ways To Turn Author Visits into Valuable Learning Experiences

Mary Francis Shura

— Betty Ren Wright, author of
GETTING RID OF MARJORIE

A good author-related school program does not begin with the arrival of the author. The author's visit is the culminating event which completes weeks of preparation by your committee and the development of exciting projects by students and teachers.

I am now going to tell you ways to get the most for your money while providing the finest in learning experiences for your students. These methods will turn a one-day event into exciting two- or three-week explorations for your teachers and students. By utilizing authors' visits as catalysts for initiating creative projects, their books will become more meaningful to teachers and students.

More, Better and Best

When authors are invited to speak to classes, they have every right to assume that students are familiar with their books and are informed about the body of work they have produced. Authors should not be expected to spend valuable time in acquainting students with their books by having to go through a series of "and then I wrotes."

Back in my "dark ages," when I first began speaking to classes, very few students had any idea who I was or what I had written. After being introduced, I would stand before students who seemed to stare at me with square eyeballs and blank expressions, wondering: "What's he going to tell us that we don't want to hear, and what's he going to show us that we don't want to see?"

Many of the teachers hadn't read my books either. Sometimes a teacher would say: "I started reading your latest book last night. Of course, I've only read a few pages, but I know I'm going to like it."

Talking to students about books they hadn't read was very unrewarding and unnerving. By day's end, I'd return home exhausted. I finally swore

— Barbara Cohen, author of
UNICORNS IN THE RAIN

I'd never step foot inside another school, and for a long time, I didn't.

Then about eight years ago, I was invited to Wentzville, Missouri, to present a full week of programs in the grade schools. I accepted because, quite frankly, I needed the money.

Although the coordinator told me that the teachers and students were very excited about my scheduled visit, I could hardly have imagined what an experience awaited me. How could I have known that five days at Wentzville would change my attitudes and approaches to speaking to classes.

It started at the front door of the first school. In the main hallway, a banner was strung from wall to wall, proclaiming: "WELCOME, MR. MELTON!" My visit was celebrated throughout every hallway and over-flowed into every classroom with displays of posters, murals, mobiles, shadow boxes, puppets and other creative projects. Each class was familiar with at least two of my books because every teacher had read some books aloud to the students and the students had read other books themselves. Some had read as many as six. And every class had developed at least two projects based on my books, resulting in the displays on walls and tables. I soon realized that I had entered a "literary circus" of one of the most innovative exhibits of student projects I had ever seen. I loved it!

Questions from students were thoughtful, astute, challenging and wonderful! Each one of my presentations went better than the one before.

At the end of the first day, I should have been tired, but I wasn't. I was higher than a kite, full of energy and enthusiasm, and eager to return the next day. The whole week was amazing — each day better than the day before. The excitement was electric.

As I drove home that weekend, I wasn't the least bit fatigued. Instead, I was bursting with energy as if my batteries had been recharged.

The Author Is the Icing, But Not the Cake

During that week, I learned that the teachers who had organized the programs in Wentzville had been students of Nancy Polette. Not long after, Nancy asked me to speak at her Writer's Conference at the Linden-wood Colleges in St. Charles, Missouri. When I mentioned how impressed I was with the organization and the wonderful projects at Wentzville and that I understood she had been instrumental in the development of such thoughtful programming, she said a very interesting thing:

"A visiting author," Nancy explained, "should never be expected to be anything but the 'icing on the cake.' Through preparation of projects in anticipation of an author's visit, teachers and students 'bake the cake.' The better the 'cake,' the more the 'icing' will be appreciated and enjoyed."

Her statement made an impact on me and dynamically changed my criteria for accepting speaking engagements. No longer do I try to supply the "cake" for such functions!

To insure that classes are properly prepared for my visits, I insist on the following:

1. Students and teachers must be aware of my background and have an overall view of my published works.

2. Students must experience at least two of my books, either through reading them or by hearing them read aloud in class.

3. Each class must prepare at least two projects based on my books.

Now, when teachers or librarians contact me to speak at their schools, I stipulate my conditions. Most teachers and librarians respond with, "That sounds like a great idea! Our students and teachers will really love this!"

When I hear such a response, I know I have found the right school for me, and I am eager to see what fascinating creative projects will be developed. I am rarely disappointed. Ninety-nine percent of the time I am rewarded with well-prepared, enthusiastic students and an array of exciting creativity.

Over the years, only a few people have grumbled, "Well, that sounds like an awful lot of work to me. I'm not sure our teachers would want to do that much." When I hear such reactions, I quickly agree that it is indeed a lot of work and suggest they contact another author — one who doesn't insist on such extensive preparation.

Some may feel I am too dictatorial in insisting on certain conditions. I may be, but my conditions provide a well-thought-out method for accelerating student awareness of written works. More precisely, they insure the success of author-related programs.

— Avi, author of
NIGHT JOURNEYS

Provide Teachers with Biographical and Bibliographical Materials

In order to give your teachers necessary information about the visiting author, request that a copy of the author's biography and a bibliography of his or her published works be sent to you.

What if the author or publisher does not provide these materials?

If the author or publisher will not prepare the materials for you, you have the choice of finding another author or preparing the information yourself by referring to his or her books in the library.

Should we insist that the author or publisher send this information?

I would. Providing such materials is a matter of professional courtesy and good common sense.

How soon should we request the author's biography and a bibliography?

Immediately upon agreement of the author's visit. You will need the information a couple of months before the event to prepare news releases and the author's introduction. At least one month before the scheduled event, be sure to distribute copies of the biography and bibliography to teachers.

Should we distribute copies of both only to teachers of participating classes?

No. Distribute copies to **all** teachers in the buildings where the author is to speak. Some of the other teachers will not only read the guest author's

What's In a Name?

When I was invited to speak at a nearby school, I mentioned to the teacher that the session would be more interesting if some of the children had read my work. She assured me they were familiar with my books.

When I found the classroom, I saw that my books were not on display. Instead, the books of the *late* Miriam Clark Potter were lined up in the chalk tray. Without attempting to be an imposter, I carried on as best I could for a disappointed third grade. The teachers said the children would like autographs, so I signed a lot of scraps of paper.

On my way out of the building, I stopped at the library, where none of my books were cataloged.

It was a humiliating experience. Even with speed reading, I think the teacher should have noticed the difference between the name, Miriam Clark Potter, and my name, Marian Potter.

— Marian Potter, author of
BLATHERSKITE

— Karen Kerber,
author and illustrator of
WALKING IS WILD,
WEIRD AND WACKY

Properly Prepared Students Make the Difference

I've had a number of programs that went well, simply because the teachers took the time to prepare the students. If that is not done, the visit is a waste of time, for them and for me.

— Theodore Taylor, author of
THE MALDONADO MIRACLE

books themselves, but will read them to their classes, too, allowing their students to at least know something about the scheduled guest.

Students Should Experience At Least Two of the Author's Books

At least two months before the author's visit, order as many copies of the author's books as you can afford and arrange to borrow as many as possible from other schools and libraries. Teachers and students will need these books for classroom use, at least one month before the author arrives.

With added emphasis on the invited author's books, teachers will find many students will read several books by the author, aside from those presented in class. Some students, for the first time, will read a complete book on their own and some will read a book that is two or three grade levels above anything they have read before.

A Time for New and Exciting Discoveries

Once you have selected your author or authors, an automatic urgency to read and review their books is generated in your school. When students realize that they are reading or hearing the books of someone they will soon meet, they pay even closer attention and begin to analyze the materials with heightened curiosity and awareness. And knowing that a visiting author will actually see their creative endeavors, students, along with their teachers, are motivated to put forth their best efforts.

So it becomes a time of new and exciting discoveries. With bursts of creativity, the excitement builds during brainstorming sessions and the subsequent development of student projects!

The Importance of Reading Aloud

Because it is impossible to have a copy of every book for each student, many teachers read the books to their classes. If scheduling an author to come into your school does nothing more than encourage teachers to spend more time reading aloud to students, it is worth all the work and the cost.

Reading aloud to students is one of the most important times in the day. We know students' hearing vocabularies extend far beyond their reading vocabularies, so teachers can read books to students which are two, even three, grade levels above their students' reading vocabularies.

When a teacher reads aloud, students are not in a passive state, but are moved into processes of creativity. They have to imagine the setting, the characters and the action. They mentally *picture* the clothing, the buildings, and all other things related to the structure of the story.

By reading aloud to students, we also increase their **writing abilities**. My experience in teaching professional and student writing courses convinced me that most people write what they **hear**, not what they **read**. I have no doubt, with the implant of better forms of literature in the students' **hearing** language, that we are expanding their choices in **writing** that language.

Students in the 1930s and 40s had a certain advantage over the students today because they listened to radio dramas. Although television offers a great deal of visual information, it does "spoon-feed" the passive viewer and offers little toward the development of the imagination. So reading aloud to students is even more important today.

For any teacher who loves books, what a splendid opportunity he or she has in becoming the voice to the words of favorite authors. I never hear or think of the book, LASSIE COME HOME, without hearing the voice of my third-grade teacher and suddenly picturing her sitting before our class in a navy blue and white polka dot dress, wiping tears from her eyes. I can think of nothing that would have pleased Miss Shelton more than to think her students would so closely associate her with such a wonderful book.

Use an Author's Work As a Springboard for Creativity

Before I visit a school, I always assist teachers in initiating creative projects by sending them a list of appropriate books, which also contains a description of each work. Recommended grade levels are presented and suggestions are offered regarding types of projects their classes might enjoy. These suggested projects did not originate with me, but are a compilation of successful activities I have seen and enjoyed in a number of schools.

Review and Adapt

It should also be noted that these suggestions are offered to be used only as *starters* to motivate students. Happily, most classes discuss them and then come up with even better and more innovative ideas of their own.

While reviewing the following list based on my books, it should be obvious that these approaches could be applied with any author's works.

RECOMMENDED BOOKS AND SUGGESTED CLASS PROJECTS

A BOY CALLED HOPELESS

A Biography   Grades 3 through 12

The story of a brain-injured boy, told from the viewpoint of his fourteen-year-old sister, M.J.

Because the narrative is written in a conversational tone, this is a wonderful book for reading aloud to the class. The humor, drawn from the experiences of the family, adds to the poignancy of the story.

Suggested Class Projects:

- Discuss problems of handicapped people.

- Students interview a handicapped person and write a paper.

- Invite a handicapped person to visit and speak to the class.

- Have right-handed students attempt activities using only the left and vice versa.

Total Agreement

I ceased having problems when I began taking more control of the previsit arrangements. I set limits as to grade levels and number of sessions per day, and I made certain that all the details were clearly understood ahead of time.

— Lynn Hall, author of
THE LEAVING

— Hilary Milton, author of
THE BRATS AND MR. JACK

Students Synthesize Author's Works

In the last school event I attended, the students had written one more chapter to one of my books, imagining what happened *after* the book's end. In another class, they wrote book reviews — all favorable. I think creative effort is always fun to hear and read. I also recall the wonderful efforts of the Philadelphia librarians when I was there — most gratifying — they *love* children's authors there.

— Paula Hendrich, author of
SAVING AMERICA'S BIRDS

- Keeping safety precautions in mind, for a period of time, have students manipulate crutches and function while sitting in a wheelchair.

THEODORE

A Novel   Grades 7 through 12

When Etta Pearson, a seventy-two-year-old woman, receives the message that her brother Theodore is seriously ill, she feels the urgent need to travel to him. As she seeks assistance from other members of her family, their strained relationships are revealed and the mystery of Theodore begins to unfold. Readers realize the characters' pasts and presents are being drawn into a collision course.

Since the location of the book is set in Missouri and Kansas, special significance is added to readers residing in the Midwest

Suggested Class Projects:

- Implement a study of family relationships.

- Discuss the development of conflict in family relationships.

- Explore problems faced by young people.

- Examine problems faced by older people.

- Discuss reactions to brain injury and mental illness.

- Discuss responsibilities of family members to each other.

- Students interview a grandparent or an elderly person in the neighborhood and write a brief biography.

- Students draw or paint their favorite scenes or characters.

THE ONE AND ONLY AUTOBIOGRAPHY OF RALPH MILLER — THE DOG WHO KNEW HE WAS A BOY

An Hilarious Thriller!   Grades 2 through 10

RALPH MILLER is an extremely funny book! The story can be enjoyed by children and adults alike. Younger children love the premise and enjoy Ralph's adventures. Older readers appreciate the currents of satire.

One of the most fascinating aspects of Ralph is that HE THINKS! Throughout the book his thought processes and his quick sense of humor are instructive without ever becoming didactic. The situations Ralph experiences can lead to group discussions about human foibles, problem solving, ethics, race relations, family unity, role playing, respecting rules, peaceful dissent, establishing lifetime goals, the news media, kidnapping, being held hostage, social structures, use and misuse of authority — in fact, the list is almost endless.

Suggested Class Projects:

- Students write sequels.

- Students write stories about what would happen if their own pets decided they were people.

- Students list the parables and clichés expressed in the book and discuss the meaning of each.

- Students draw illustrations of favorite characters.

Students Should Be Familiar with Author's Books

Most of all, see that the children are familiar with the books...or even one of them. It could even be a book the teacher has read to the class. It's so much more interesting for everyone if the contents of the books are known and some questions are prepared ahead of time.

— Stella Pevsner, author of
  I'LL ALWAYS REMEMBER YOU,
  MAYBE

Presenting the Basics

It might be well for teachers to explain to the children beforehand, just what a writer or illustrator does, and maybe touch on the rudiments of printing. So many times we have such questions as: "How do you put the covers on?" and "Who puts the words in the books?" and "How do you put the pictures in?"

— Clyde Robert Bulla, author of
  CONQUISTA

- Students construct mobiles, make puppets, create slide series.

- Students present scenes from the book as one-act plays. (Because the dialogue is so complete, the scenes can be easily acted out, complete with costumes.)

IMAGES OF GREATNESS
An Illustrated Anthology   Grades 2 through College

Features 46 illustrations and over 190 quotations of senior citizens who have made major contributions to the world.

Suggested Class Projects:

- Students write and illustrate a brief biography about a noted person.

- Students interview a grandparent or elderly person, then write and illustrate a biography.

- Students research five interesting facts about a selected person.

- Students draw self-portraits and write about one lifetime goal they would attempt to achieve in order to become future "Images of Greatness."

AND GOD CREATED...
A Picture Book   Grades K through 12

A retelling of the story of the Creation according to Genesis, done in illustration and free verse.

May or may not be presented in a religious context. Many teachers in public schools present the book as a work of art to stimulate fresh approaches to drawing and painting.

Suggested Class Projects:

- Students develop paintings and drawings of the universe and the world being created.

- Stimulate a study of the universe by presenting the book.

- Students retell other well-known stories in their own words and illustrate these stories.

HARRY S. TRUMAN —
THE MAN WHO WALKED WITH GIANTS
Historical Biography   Grades 4 through College

The life and times of the thirty-third president of the United States literally vibrates on the pages of this informative and elaborately illustrated book. The narrative is selective and clearly stated. The unique format features brief biographies of other world leaders and associates, and numerous historical events are further explained in footnotes. Forty-six full-color illustrations and over sixty pencil drawings provide visual excitement.

Once you review the book's unique format and vivid illustrations, you will understand why teachers are so excited about presenting it to students on such a wide range of grade levels.

Student Preparation Sets the Stage

Certain teachers and librarians consistently prepare their students better than others, and there is a direct correlation between the impact of my presentation and the way the students have been prepared.

— Robert C. Lee, author of
IT'S A MILE
FROM HERE TO GLORY

Time To Spare, Money To Burn!

The closest thing to a horror story occurred at one school (and it was costly for the school) in which I saw one group of twelve students and another group of fifteen students, none of whom knew why they had come to the library or who I was until I introduced myself. That was the extent of my responsibilities, for which the school paid my honorarium, plus overnight accommodations, plus $350.00 for air fare. Such a waste!

— Barbara Robinson, author of
THE BEST CHRISTMAS
PAGEANT EVER

Suggested Class Projects:

- Develop a time scale of Truman's life.

- Students write and illustrate a major contribution of Truman or an event in his life.

- Each student selects a different president, draws an illustration and writes a brief biography. Compile a book using these materials.

- Discuss which decisions made by Truman influenced history and are still affecting today's events.

- Students write themes exploring and comparing the similarities and differences in Truman's childhood with those of today's students.

- Students select favorite statements by Truman, write comments on them, then illustrate their papers.

Projects Can Expand the Learning Experiences of Students

What wonderful projects could be created, based on Jean George's MY SIDE OF THE MOUNTAIN, or Thomas Rockwell's HOW TO EAT FRIED WORMS, or Willo Roberts's GIRL WITH THE SILVER EYES, and the books of many other writers.

The works of most authors can be easily utilized in motivating students' creative projects. Such projects increase and expand the quality of learning experiences.

For Individual and Group Projects, Students Can:

- Create murals.

- Write and perform plays, complete with costumes and scenery.

- Build a puppet stage, create puppets, and write and perform puppet plays.

- Create room decorations.

- Compile a book composed of writings and illustrations submitted by all the students, then bind these materials together.

- Do drawings of characters or scenes from a selected book.

- Create a three-dimensional scene in a shoebox.

- Make papier-mache figures.

- Mold clay figures.

- Design book covers.

- Make posters.

- Write and illustrate original stories or sequels to selected books.

- Write, illustrate and construct original books.

All of these suggested projects offer students opportunities to extract

The Responsibility of Teachers

First and foremost, the children must have read at least two of the writer's books. This depends on the teachers and it is their responsibility.

— Julia Cunningham, author of
THE TREASURE IS THE ROSE

— Jean Craighead George, author of
JULIE OF THE WOLVES

concepts from the author's materials, then to develop their own creative ideas. Not only do students read and enjoy the visiting author's books, but they can create new and exciting pieces of writing and artwork based on the author's work. Personal involvement of the students makes the author's visit mutually rewarding — the authors see the wonderful ideas their books have generated in students and the students love the opportunity to show their creative efforts to visiting authors.

Our goals as teachers and authors go beyond filling students' heads with facts. More importantly, when we affect their thinking processes, students are able to analyze and rearrange facts and ignite their own creativity.

How should teachers select the types of class projects?

Let the students decide. Have brainstorming sessions. Let the students develop a list of exciting projects and vote on which two they would like to create.

Motivate, Initiate, Innovate!

Remember, the scheduled author and his or her books become valuable motivating factors. They offer students reasons to create. Your students will want to please their guest. They won't feel they are writing or drawing for just another grade score, but for someone special who is going to see the results of their work. The quality of their writing and drawing will improve before your eyes.

As the projects begin to take shape, the students in each class are going to be very interested in the projects being developed by other classes. When students see an exceptionally exciting project across the hall, don't be surprised if their own projects become even more creative. Classes become very competitive in their creations, each striving to outdo the others.

The bursts of enthusiasm and activities are like Christmas, Halloween and the Fourth of July rolled into one. Hallways become three-ring circuses of color and imagination — all related to the books of the scheduled author. It's terrific! Your teachers and students will love it! And you will be pleasantly surprised at how very interested parents become in the projects and the arrival of the author.

When properly planned and developed, your author-related school program can become one of the best learning experiences and public relations events of the year.

— David McAdoo,
author and illustrator of
THE DRAGON OF ORD

Mrs. Little Local Author

Once upon a time, a little local author was invited to visit two classrooms at a little local school. When she arrived, it became immediately apparent that only the principal was expecting her and that he had told no one of her imminent arrival. Instead, he marched her into the first classroom, interrupting the teacher's lesson, much to the teacher's surprise and the class's confusion, and said, "This is Mrs. Little Local Author. She's going to talk to you about her books." Then he left. Twenty minutes later, he returned, led Little Local to the next class and pulled the same stunt again.

Some people say the third time's the charm. This man will never know.

— Sandy Asher, author of
   TEDDY TEABURY'S
   FABULOUS FACT

STOP THE PRESSES!
START THE CAMERAS!

How To Obtain Media Coverage for Author-Related Programs

Wilma Pitchford Hays

— Tomie dePaola,
author and illustrator of
STREGA NONA

Scheduling authors to speak at programs is newsworthy. But don't expect newsreporters and camera crews to beat on the doors of your school, because they won't. If you want to obtain news coverage for your event, you have to plan ahead and work for it.

**Is getting media coverage
worth the time and effort?**

You bet it is! Let's face it — your school, any school, needs all the positive public relations it can get. When SAT scores drop a few points, newsreporters will blaze headlines across front pages and television will harbinger the news on prime time. But, get the scores up and you'll be lucky to find an article on page 17 of the town's chronicle and TV camera crews will be out chasing fire engines. Although it shouldn't be that way, reporters too often rely on their adage: "Bad News Is Good News. Good News Is Boring!"

In many communities, author-related school programs are readily reported by television and newspapers; in others they won't even be noticed. I am convinced that the difference is not due to aggressive editors and station managers, but in how well the communities have informed and prepared the media to cover the events.

Now Hear This!

If you want the very best news coverage for your program, I advise you to get Rosemary Lumsden to handle your public relations or find someone like her — which may be near to impossible because I've never met anyone quite like Rosemary. She's an extraordinary and unique person who really cares about the students and teachers in her community and, as a parent volunteer, helps organize wonderful programs in southeastern

— Shel Silverstein,
author and illustrator of
THE GIVING TREE

Good-bye, Fresno, Good-bye!

One of my worst experiences was a two-day visit to some schools in Fresno. Without our written consent, the program organizers had scheduled us for eight sessions, back to back, with a scant half-hour lunch period and nonexistent breaks. They didn't seem to realize that no one, having lived through this ordeal, would ever come back.

— Julia Cunningham, author of
THE TREASURE IS THE ROSE

Missouri. She seeks out and obtains the finest news coverage for these school programs because she thoroughly understands how the media works and how to present information to them…and when.

Since Rosemary's services are not for hire throughout the country, I asked her to write the following tips and observations. I urge you and your committee members to read and consider them carefully, then go ye and do likewise.

How To Obtain the Best Media Coverage

by Rosemary Lumsden

An effective publicity campaign begins long before the actual event takes place. A publicity person or committee needs to think of all possible ways to build media value in the upcoming event.

The first step is to convince the media — the newspapers, radio and television stations — that the event is important enough to occupy media space and time. Editors and broadcasters are not lacking for stories to fill their newspapers and air waves. If you want your publicity to reach the public, you must be prepared to compete by making your story more newsworthy and interesting than the other items crossing the editor's desk.

Prepare a News Release

A good news release is direct and to the point. For example:

News Release

On October 16, 1987, George Bernard Twain, noted author of juvenile books, will speak to the fifth- and sixth-grade classes at Sunnyvale Elementary School, 1780 N. Cherry Hill Drive.

All classes have read books by Mr. Twain and, in his honor, have developed exciting creative projects related to the author's books, and these projects will be on display.

Students and teachers are very enthusiastic and eager to meet one of their favorite authors.

We will be happy to arrange time for one of your reporters to interview Mr. Twain and participating students and teachers. And we will assist your photographer and/or camera crew in photographing the planned activities.

Enclosed is a copy of Mr. Twain's biography and a bibliography of his books.

Please contact Publicity and Public Relations Coordinator:

Ida Gotcha
Sunnyvale Elementary School
1780 N. Cherry Hill Drive
Ohmygosh, NE 66828
(498) 632-0048

Tips for Preparing News Releases

- All materials should be neatly typed and double-spaced.

- Give the "Who, What, When, Where and Why" facts and make sure they're accurate. You can easily lose your credibility if your news release brings calls of "correction please!" from readers/listeners.

- If you're doing advance publicity, check with the media to see how far in advance they want the news release.

- When reporting names of students participating in an event, the media like to give their age, "son (or daughter) of ", and the name of their hometown.

- Be timely. If it's worth reporting, it's worth reporting at the time of the event! Newspapers don't like stale news and broadcasters completely ignore it!

- If your press release is longer than one page, type the word (MORE) at the bottom of each page except the last. At the end, type "-30-" or "END".

- Be sure to include your name, address, phone number and a topic heading on all press releases. An editor, needing to ask you a question, may hold up the printing of your story for want of a single important detail.

- Press releases to radio stations should be *short*, neatly typed and double-spaced, all in capital letters.

- Public service announcements for radio should run thirty or sixty seconds — no longer. (Thirty-second spots are often preferred.)

Special Considerations

I like to follow up large-group presentations, which are relatively formal, with visits with smaller groups. I especially enjoy working with small groups of children who have special needs — those who are deaf, gifted, dyslexic, or retarded. I also enjoy meeting groups of kids who have a special interest in writing. I prefer that these be children who appoint themselves for the meeting because in all my years in public schools, not one of my teachers knew I was a writer. It is ideal when teachers and administrators in a school take an interest in my visit, too, and even ask questions.

— Jane Resh Thomas, author of
THE PRINCESS IN THE PIGPEN

Don't Hesitate
To Write the Story, Yourself

I have been quite fortunate to learn from the managing editor of our city's newspaper. I began taking news releases to him in 1984 to announce a writer's workshop. Knowing details are sometimes confused or omitted when the story is given verbally to a busy reporter, I wrote the articles myself.

The fact that I considered the event important enough to write about it myself stirred the editor's interest. I later found this true with several newspapers to which I submitted news releases. Although news releases may be edited and rearranged, if you properly prepare them so they require minimal revision, your original versions stand a greater chance of being printed.

For Human Consumption

To make a story initially appealing to readers/editors, the guest author's name and a description and purpose of your event need to appear early

— Byrd Baylor, author of
THE DESERT IS THEIRS

What Can One Do?

A school librarian from a nearby suburb coaxed me into coming to her school. When the children came into the learning center, they asked the woman who I was and why I was there. We were seated in a circle, and as I talked, the kids were talking, too, until I finally stopped and asked if they'd just rather talk to each other. The woman made no effort to control them. Afterwards, though, she talked and talked to me, and I had the distinct impression that she had just wanted to meet me, herself.

— Anonymous

— Patricia MacLachlan, author of
    ARTHUR,
    FOR THE VERY FIRST TIME

in the story. From there, your task is to **hold** their attention! The method that has worked for me is to write the body of the story, telling the human interest details of the event.

Another lesson I learned in preparing publicity for newspapers was to stay away from educational jargon.

"How many of our readers know what an 'adjunct professor' is?" my editor would ask me. "And how many know what 'learning modalities' or 'psycholinguistics' are? How many even care?"

Unless the wording has meaning for the layman, I no longer quote from the biographies provided by authors or publishers. If I can't put the information into everyday language, I leave it out. Once I learned this lesson, my publicity articles graduated to the point of little or no editing and began to appear on page 2 instead of page 7 or 8.

Get the Picture!

Photographs help draw attention to your article. If possible, get a local person in a picture with your celebrity for advance publicity; this helps to build interest. Pictures of local people, taken while they are talking to the author at the event you are publicizing, give recognition to people in your community, which is what both you and the editor want. So have someone there with a good camera and black and white film, even if you must hire a professional photographer. When you give an editor something to make his or her paper more interesting to readers, you are building media value in the project you are publicizing, as well as building your own credibility with the editor.

Utilizing the Services of Publicity Departments

If the school or college where your event is being held has an effective office of news services, you may find that working with them is helpful. I have worked with the coordinators of news services at a number of colleges and universities. I provide the coordinators with pertinent information and tell them which day and time will be good for taking pictures. They take pictures, making a record of the names of individuals in each picture, then write the press releases and have the stories, with pictures, in the hands of editors in less than a week.

Suggest Times for Interviews and Photography Sessions

If you provide them with information at least a week ahead of time, local newspapers and television stations will usually send a reporter to cover your event. You may also be able to interest local radio stations. Send a printed biography and a bibliography on your visiting author, and give enough newsworthy details about the event and list local persons who will participate — the five Ws again — to convince the media that it will be interesting to the public.

When sending advance notices to the press, I suggest the best times during which reporters can get the most interesting pictures and interviews. You should analyze the schedule of your event and pick out those times when you think the activities will be in full swing and will make for the most interesting pictures. It will be extremely helpful if these activity times are close to an open hour (not a break time) so the guest speaker is available for an interview.

It's a neat trick to bring it all together — the activity, the guest author, the students, the reporters and the photographer. When it works, it's like magic. When it doesn't, it means that you may have to quickly adjust some time frames. Such adjustments often have to be made because rarely are reporters on time, and when they arrive, they usually expect everything to stop and start on their schedules. Your key for getting the best news coverage may rely on your quick appraisals and ready adjustments.

Remember To Remind the Media

Be sure to call newspapers, radio and television stations a day or two prior to your event to remind them of the schedule. A courteous offer of "Would you like any further information?" is probably a better approach than to indicate that you thought they might have forgotten your event.

Always Update Your Materials

When reporters arrive, hand them copies of the author's biography and a bibliography, and an updated news release, describing the event in total. This makes the reporters' jobs easier and helps to assure accuracy in their news stories.

Be Informative, Cooperative and Friendly!

By being friendly and working closely with the news media, you will be able to reduce the time required to accomplish what you both want — favorable recognition of the author's visit and excellent public relations for your school.

Good News Is Good News!

Good publicity is an important part of any author-related school program. Make certain the person handling the publicity is aware of this importance and is interested enough to do the job. Courtesy toward the press and a genuine respect for their time are essential in gaining the coverage you desire. Offer news to the media that is of value to them, and you will get the coverage for your author-related programs.

— Leonard Wibberly, author of
THE MOUSE THAT ROARED

I Shall Not Return

My worst day was one where nine sessions were scheduled instead of my requested six. The overhead didn't work, class after class arrived without pencils and paper, and there hadn't been a quarter of a second of preparation on the students' behalf. The students simply came to school, then they were lined up and marched to the library for an "unknown" assembly. To make matters worse, the principal decided to use my time to hold conferences with her teachers. I will never return to this school.

— Greg Denman, author of
WHEN YOU'VE MADE IT YOUR OWN
— Teaching Poetry to Young People

What We Do
and What We Are

It takes much more energy to perform than most people assume. We give our hard-learned techniques.

We are consultants, not teachers.

The Canadians asked endless, probing questions about my style, the characters and culture, and my motivations and philosophies that compelled me to present given incidents. My, but I've never witnessed such sincere interest in and appreciation for literature, and I did not feel it was done for me alone, but for themselves. What a joy!

— Berniece Rabe, author of
   NAOMI

7

"HAVE YOU HEARD, MY CAT HAD SIX KITTENS?"

How To Prepare Students To Ask Proper Questions

During an author's visit, teachers seem to be more concerned with the quality of questions their students will ask the author than almost anything else. If students ask their guest thoughtful questions, their teacher beams with pride. But if questions are poor, or even worse, silly, their teacher's day hits rock bottom.

If this book does no more than lessen such tensions, it will have been worth the writing and the reading.

How can we best prepare students to ask proper questions?

If students have experienced at least two of the author's books and have developed at least two related projects, I guarantee that they will have a successful meeting with the author. Without prodding or prompting, students will be loaded with good comments and questions.

Instead of urging students to ask predetermined questions, teachers should simply let students know they are free to ask whatever they wish. Unless the natural instincts of students have been squelched, they are born questioners. Give them the freedom to ask what comes naturally.

To insure the best questions will be asked, should we have students write them in advance?

Not if I'm coming to your school! When I am faced with students reading questions, I immediately stop and have them put away their notes. Having students read from prepared questionnaires makes for the dullest type of interaction. Many students will reread their own questions to themselves instead of listening to the author's answers. "Spontaneity" is the word for the day.

Their prepared questions often have little or no regard for the presentation the author has just made. An author may have just finished talking about his or her last book, and some student will read: "What is the title

— Peter Parnall,
author and illustrator of
THE MOUNTAIN

— Raboo Rodgers, author of
MAGNUM FAULT

Students Know How
To Beat the System

Students beat the system by asking two questions, and usually in this exact order:

"How old were you when your first book was published?"

"How long ago was your first book published?"

As soon as answers are given, some students will add the second figure to the first, and the grand total is quickly whispered from person to person. Rest assured, by the end of the session, every student in the room knows the author's age.

— David Melton, author of
WRITTEN & ILLUSTRATED BY...

of your most recent book?" In mutual response, the other students groan, and even the questioner realizes the question makes him or her appear dumb.

Should we have students
bring pencil and paper for taking notes?

I hope not. This is a personal opinion, but I would rather talk with relaxed students. I don't like them to feel as if they are preparing for a test. Besides, I like to see their faces, not the tops of their heads.

Are there any questions
students should not ask a visiting author?

There are two questions students are usually warned not to ask and some authors prefer not to be asked:

"How much money do you make?" and

"How old are you?"

Neither question bothers me. I am sometimes alone in this opinion, but I happen to think both questions are good ones and deserve to be answered.

To begin with, I find even very young children are interested in money and are curious to know how well creative people are paid.

As for asking about age, I realize there's a gentlemen's and a ladies' social agreement that adults are not to be asked how old they are. That's obviously an adult rule — no kid would ever have invented such a thing. And it's not a very good rule because it projects a double standard.

When we adults meet children, the first things we ask them, are:

"What is your name?" and

"How old are you?"

Although we allow children to ask adults their names, we forbid them to inquire about our ages. I think such a rule cheats children of a very important piece of comparative information in life. If they are not allowed to ask, how are they going to learn what people look like at thirty years of age, and at forty, or fifty, or sixty, and so on?

However, since this firmly established double standard is maintained by adults, unfair or not, it is probably a good idea for teachers to remind students that many adults do not like to be asked their ages. And while they're at it, teachers should probably remind students not to ask the money question either. Explain it as you will, children will see it as unfair and rather silly — and I think they are right!

In summary, I suppose the best advice, is:

Within the standards of good taste and social acceptance, students should be allowed to ask any question. If the author doesn't wish to answer a particular question, he or she has the right to refuse or to change the subject.

Is it all right for teachers to prompt
students to ask certain questions?

It is usually better to leave students alone. But if the teacher has a question he or she wants answered, then the teacher should do the asking.

Teachers should exercise some caution about entering the conversation. If the question and answer session is going well, it is often better for teachers to reserve their questions until the end. Sometimes when a teacher interjects a question, the students suddenly "clam up" and stop asking their questions. That can really squelch a good session.

Should we instruct students as to the best way to ask questions?

Yes. Instruct your students to take turns and ask only one question at a time. It is most helpful to the speaker if students raise their hands only between answers and not keep waving them in the air while the author is trying to talk.

How much time should be allowed for question and answer sessions?

Normally ten minutes is sufficient. No matter how good are the questions or how interesting are the author's answers, students may become restless if this period is overextended.

Should time always be allowed for questions?

I think time for questions should be allowed. If students are prepared to ask questions, they feel cheated if they're not given the opportunity.

Should teachers discuss types of questions before students meet with the author?

Yes, but don't overdo it. If the author makes a good presentation and if students are familiar with the author's works, the students will automatically have questions to ask.

As teachers, we are trained to answer questions and make concluding statements, but some restraint should be shown in answering too many questions for students before the author arrives. Instead of giving an immediate answer, when a student asks a question in class about the author or his or her work, the teacher might suggest that that question would be a good one to ask the author.

What if students don't ask the author anything, but later, they barrage their teacher with questions?

You schedule a firing squad at sunrise — what else?

Seriously, this can be really annoying and it sometimes happens for no apparent reason. The author is pleasant and friendly, the students are well prepared and very interested, yet no one offers to ask questions. Then as soon as the session is finished and the classes return to their rooms, the students start asking their teacher the questions they should have asked the author. This situation most often presents itself in the upper grades where peer pressure has enormous influence. But I don't know anyone who can keep second or third graders from asking questions, anytime and anywhere.

To avoid "question" problems, my best advice is to introduce your students to the author's books, have them create wonderful projects, be sure to get them to the session on time, and then allow the chemistry between the author and the students to develop as it will.

The Ego Buster of the Day

Once I was launched into a presentation to a group of youngsters, and after about twenty minutes, I decided to take a deep breath and ask if there were any questions so far. A little boy waved his hand with great vigor, so I called on him expecting a deeply meaningful question about my writing.

"What's your name?" the youngster asked.

— Robert C. Lee, author of
IT'S A MILE
FROM HERE TO GLORY

— Maia Rodman, author of
SHADOW OF A BULL

Questions, Please!

For me, it used to be a kind of nightmare when the kids just sat there and wouldn't talk, wouldn't respond. I soon learned that I'd better have enough stories on tap to fill a time period — just in case.

— Clyde Robert Bulla, author of
CONQUISTA

The Way It Should Be

In Louisiana, Missouri, the librarian had sold copies of my books prior to my speaking engagement. In addition, by the time I arrived at the school, all the teachers had discussed and/or read one of my books to their classes. The children were familiar with my work and filled with questions to ask me. Posters and related art projects were made before my visit and many of the children had written books and poems to share with me. A lovely lunch, away from the school, was planned, which gave me a chance to meet other people in the school district and to have a brief change of pace.

The enthusiasm for me was inspired by their familiarity with my books, which is always a wonderful boost for a writer. It gave me a chance to laugh with the children about various scrapes my characters inevitably found themselves in and to discuss the ideas on which my books are based.

— Jan Greenberg, author of
    NO DRAGONS TO SLAY

Peter Zachary Cohen

8

IF YOU DON'T BEHAVE, WE'LL . . . !

Proper and Courteous Behavior Expected from Everyone

"Make us proud of you," parents and teachers tell students before a visitor arrives.

Adults are usually apprehensive that students will not put their best feet forward. We want them to sit down, be quiet, and listen attentively. Nothing wrong with that! Proper behavior should be expected.

If students don't learn good manners at home or at school, where will they learn them? Certainly not at football games or rock concerts.

Setting Examples, Reviewing the Rules

How should we prepare students to exhibit their best behavior and manners for our guest?

The same way we prepare children to greet visitors in our homes. Common courtesies and politeness are not developed in a one-day crash course. They are developed by example and through experience.

In those households where visitors are commonplace and where parents have stressed gracious and cordial behavior to their children, proper greetings and attention are readily offered to guests.

If your classes have a number of guest speakers in their rooms, students have opportunities to practice good manners. If these opportunities are few, students are at a disadvantage. So teachers should take the responsibility of discussing the aspects of proper behavior:

"How do you do?"

"I'm pleased to meet you."

"We really like your books."

"Yes, Ma'ams" and "No, Sirs" may be considered old-fashioned by many, but these terms of address are still nice to hear in a civilized world.

— Jack Prelutsky, author of
THE SNOPP ON THE SIDEWALK

Visiting Authors Face Everchanging Surroundings

Authors know how many hours a teacher teaches, but what we do is *not* the same thing. We are not on our home ground. We do not know the kids or what they're liable to do at any moment. We cannot discipline them. We are facing hundreds of unfamiliar faces, child and adult, all day and are expected to be pleasant to all of them. The only place we can stop smiling is the restroom — *if* the stalls have doors.

— Sandy Asher, author of
    TEDDY TEABURY'S
    FABULOUS FACT

One Man's Opinion

I want: Someone to introduce me who isn't a colorless nerd, but a real crowd-warmer; an audience of working teachers (or writers) where administrators are not there to wet-blanket the atmosphere; and during my talk to kids, teachers who smile and are interested, instead of chattering to one another.

— Robert Newton Peck, author of
    A DAY NO PIGS WOULD DIE

Should we make special arrangements for students who have persistent discipline problems?

If you mean, keep them out of the sessions, the answer is, "No." I think every student, hyperactive or not, should have the opportunity to attend the sessions.

At one Children's Literature Festival, a teacher told me: "You'll be happy to know, we left all the discipline problems at the school."

I told her that didn't make me happy at all, because studies reveal that many of these kids have enormous potentials for creativity. These students, too, should have opportunities to meet creative people.

However, if a teacher knows two or three students who might be disruptive, he or she should arrange for them to be seated where they can be easily supervised, not on the other side of the room. Once a session is in progress, there is nothing worse than to have a teacher call out warnings or suddenly dash across the room to collar some student.

Although most seasoned speakers can deal with disruptive students and know how to draw them into the discussion or to quiet them, through proper planning, an alert teacher will keep such problems at a minimum.

How To Prepare Teachers To Behave Properly

The idea that teachers should be reminded of simple courtesies may seem either strange or courageous on my part (or affirm that "Fools rush in where angels fear to tread"). Be that as it may, teachers are adults and they're supposed to know how to behave when visitors arrive. Believe it or not, however, there are some (few though they may be) who either don't know proper rules of etiquette or choose to ignore them, or they consider such rules do not apply to teachers.

There are teachers who will stand back and not even greet the author at the door.

While the author is speaking, some will sit at the back of the room, or even worse, in front, and grade papers or read magazines.

Others will leave the room and return several times, slamming the door shut with every exit and entrance.

Sometimes two or three teachers will sit together and talk to each other during an entire session.

Others will frequently interrupt the speaker to offer personal views and opinions.

Or they will sit and fidget as if the author's session is keeping them from more pressing matters.

Some will not even show the courtesy of thanking the author. And perhaps worst of all — there are teachers who will sit stiffly, looking absolutely stone-faced, offering no smile of approval or frown of disapproval. They just look straight ahead, tight-lipped and dead-eyed.

Why do some teachers do these things? I don't know. Perhaps they're nervous. Maybe they're under tremendous pressures, either personal or professional. Or maybe they have strange personality quirks or whatever.

In any case, it is difficult to believe that the very people who should be most aware of the importance of proper response to a speaker are at times the rudest. And what really amazes me is that often these same people will write the most glowing evaluations of the sessions. Baffling indeed!

Please carefully and tactfully remind your teachers that they are the ones who should set proper examples for students to follow.

No one has the right to behave badly or rudely — not even visiting authors.

**Should the principal attend
at least one of the author's sessions?**

Absolutely. A principal's job is to know about the activities in the building and to evaluate the worthiness of programs. He or she can't do that from the front office. Besides, the author is a guest in the building. As head of that building's staff, the principal's attendance is a gesture of courtesy.

Don't most principals attend at least one session?

I am surprised at the number who don't. However, unless there is a real emergency, the better ones always do.

— Stanley Kiesel, author of
THE WAR BETWEEN
THE PITIFUL TEACHERS
AND THE SPLENDID KIDS

Preparing Other School Personnel for the Author's Visit

Take time to prepare **all** building personnel for the author's visit.

When authors are invited to your school, they assume they have been asked because they are wanted. Most of them know you and your committee have gone to considerable work to make such an event possible. They trust they will receive a warm welcome. They don't expect red-carpet treatment, but do hope for a genuine interest in their comfort, much as you would afford a welcome guest in your home.

Visiting authors don't expect to hear maintenance people complain about having to set up extra chairs or clean up a room. And they don't expect to receive snide comments from music teachers or physical education instructors about how the program has loused up their daily schedules.

If you, as host, and your teachers convey that an author's visit is planned and eagerly awaited, you will find that most authors will respond by presenting the finest programs possible, giving full measure and even performing beyond the call of duty. I have found most authors to be exceedingly generous people, and because they sincerely care about students, they strive very hard to please. They will do almost anything within their power to make your program a successful, long-remembered event.

Fewer Are Better

I'd rather speak to two or three small groups in a classroom or library than one large group in a cavernous auditorium.

In one small group, the girls and boys were wearing name tags. I appreciated that because I could say, "Yes, Jennifer," and "What do you think of that, Henry?" The children had been exceptionally well prepared. They had read my books. They knew something about my background. They had prepared questions and had them written down. The session with them was a pleasure.

— Clyde Robert Bulla, author of
CONQUISTA

The Rules Apply to Guest Authors Too!

**After we have made all plans, arranged schedules,
raised financing, and prepared the students and teachers,
can we expect the best behavior from our visiting author?**

You should neither expect nor accept anything less than their very best!

Presenting Both Sides

I do think, as an addenda, LIVE AUTHORS should include something about what to do when the author doesn't perform up to par — shows up inebriated or late, etc. I have heard stories of authors who were such showmen that it was impossible for a fellow author to share the platform with them as they monopolized the whole time. I guess the best advice to give in situations like these is to let the word get around that certain writers might present problems. Then program planners can decide whether these people are worth the trouble.

— Paula Hendrich, author of
SAVING AMERICA'S BIRDS

— Dav Pilkey, author of
WORLD WAR WON

An author's obligations are to relate to students and teachers in a friendly, courteous manner, give an informative presentation, display genuine interest in the work of the teachers and students, and enhance public relations for the school and community.

I think you'll find that most authors are aware of these responsibilities and will admirably fulfill their obligations.

But what if we get a real prima donna who can't be satisfied with anything?

An unfortunate situation, and while rare, it does occur.

At a recent children's gathering, one author refused to autograph paperback copies of his books because, as he said, "The low rate of royalties isn't worth the effort."

As soon as the coordinator heard about it, she discussed the problem with the author, who finally condescendingly compromised by initialing the paperbacks.

I have heard program coordinators complain about a few very well known authors who demand on being the constant center of attention. I have also heard about a couple of authors who specialize in running up large meal and drink bills at restaurants, expecting the schools to pick up the tabs.

How can we avoid such problems?

Establish limits for meals. As for drinks, I don't think any school should be expected to pay for alcoholic beverages. And most authors don't expect it. In fact, I know of many, myself included, who will not allow drinks to be placed on a meal ticket, even if the school hasn't restricted it.

Out of the hundreds of authors I have met and those whom I have followed in presenting programs, I have observed and heard of so few problems that I am convinced these difficulties are rare indeed. But let me remind you, if you get recommendations from other groups who have had experiences with the authors you wish to invite, you can probably avoid such problems.

If we have such a problem, what should we do?

First, discuss the problem with the guest author and try to resolve it. If this fails, you have the choice of making the best of a bad situation or sending the author to the principal's office. I mean that literally — someone, either the program coordinator or the school principal, should settle the problem with the author.

But what if an author becomes angry, threatens to leave, or does leave?

Let him or her leave. Although students and teachers may be terribly disappointed, such a situation does provide a valuable learning experience for students. They learn, no matter how famous or talented a person may be, that it is totally unacceptable for anyone to openly display unprofessional behavior or outright rudeness.

If an author is dismissed for improper behavior or chooses to leave under such circumstances, you have every right to consider whether or not the agreement for the author's services is null and void.

Do you mean we shouldn't pay them?

Not one peso! Bid them *adios* and farewell.

Everyone Working Together Promotes Complete Success!

Author-related school programs are designed to bring authors, teachers and students together in a congenial atmosphere that provides positive learning experiences for everyone. Discussions of the creative processes and the joys of discovery should make our cups overflow. Based on such a premise, authors, teachers and students should be receptive and courteous to each other and enjoy their meeting.

No matter how well prepared are the author's presentations or how well organized are the programs, disruptive, discourteous behavior on the part of **anyone** can spoil the day. Avoid it at all costs.

A word of warning — just because we have discussed good manners, don't overreact and issue unnecessary ultimatums to your teachers and students or be too leery of your invited author. Just take the following reasonable precautions:

- Before inviting authors, make inquiries and get recommendations.

- Use diplomacy in encouraging teachers and students to use good manners.

- Remind teachers that it is wise to attend every session with their students, not only out of courtesy, but in order to guide follow-up activities and answer questions their students may ask later.

- Encourage principals to attend at least one session.

- Prepare other building personnel to offer proper and friendly assistance.

Use Precautions and Common Sense, And Keep the Faith

Everyone should be aware that author-related school programs are established to create valuable learning experiences for students. These should be joyous events which combine enthusiasm, courtesy and the utmost cooperation from everyone — including the students, teachers, librarians, principals, maintenance personnel and authors.

When guests are present, teachers and parents want the students in their charge to be on their best behavior. We instruct them. We warn them. We even threaten them. But once the guest arrives, we must also have faith that students will come through with flying colors. And, in most cases, if we will just relax, they will "make us proud."

No author who has had experience in speaking in schools expects students to sit absolutely still like robots or teachers to sit in rapt attention every second. They do want a relaxed, friendly audience that feels free to respond and interact.

In return, students and teachers have the right to expect an eager, interested, congenial guest author.

— Bill Wallace, author of
A DOG CALLED KITTY

Judge Not Less Ye Be Judged

I come to a town as a friend, and not to evaluate or criticize anyone. And I will not be evaluated or criticized. When I die, I may be judged in Hell by Satan, or in Heaven by my God, but I'll not be judged in Yahooville! Never again will I go to that self-righteous town!

— Robert Newton Peck, author of
A DAY NO PIGS WOULD DIE

Teacher and Librarian Enthusiasm Provides Key Factor for Success

I recently visited a school in a nearby small town. Two fourth-grade girls took me around to various classrooms and introduced me with a puppet show they had written themselves. I visited briefly with first- and second-grade classes in their rooms, then spoke to an assembly of third to sixth grades.

A group of teachers took me out for a pleasant lunch in a quiet restaurant. After lunch, I spoke to two assemblies of junior and senior high students of only those students who had expressed an interest and done extra work to earn the privilege.

After school there was a tea for me and for the teachers and students who had worked to produce "Lynn Hall Day." The school had been extensively decorated, and I was presented with gifts the children had made for me.

The enthusiasm of the teachers and librarian was the key factor in this, and in all other successful speaking days.

— Lynn Hall, author of
  THE LEAVING

Jeannette Eyerly

9

MAKE YOUR LISTS, CHECK THEM TWICE!

Organizational Tips for the Final Countdown

In initiating any project or program, you shouldn't allow yourselves to be lulled by the false notion that there will be plenty of time for planning and coordinating. At best, that is only wishful thinking. To insure that everything is accomplished in proper time frames, you must begin to make lists. These lists become road maps to your final destination — a successful author-related school program.

As you compose your lists, consider the following suggestions only as *starters*. You should pick and choose those suggestions which meet your specific requirements, then add other ideas of your own.

Checklist — Two Months Before the Event

☐ Contact school and public librarians in your area about the possibility of borrowing books by your guest author.

☐ Either by phone or mail, contact the publisher or publishers of the author's books and discuss order procedures.

Most editors of juvenile and young adult books have experience in arranging such matters and are eager to help or direct you to the proper department.

Remember, you will need books for use in classrooms at least one month prior to the event and books to sell at least one week before the author arrives.

Meet with the members of your committee and discuss the following responsibilities:

— Isabelle Holland, author of
A HORSE NAMED PEACEABLE

— Robin F. Brancato, author of
FACING UP

Get Everything in Writing

My worse experience happened at an out-of-town engagement. There was a misunderstanding concerning my agreed-upon fee, which unfortunately had not been put in writing. I accepted the appointment with the impression that I was to receive a certain amount, plus traveling expenses, for a half-day appearance at one school. However, when I arrived, I was notified that I would actually be speaking to students from two schools, but they would all be in one auditorium. That was all right with me.

Although I did receive the amount agreed upon, it was for a *full* day's worth of work and I actually spoke to two schools instead of one. I also had to pay my own travel expenses. You can be sure that in the future, all transactions will be written.

— Helen R. Sattler, author of
NATURE'S WEATHER
FORECASTERS

☐ Travel and lodging for the author;

☐ Local transportation for the author;

☐ Meals for the author;

☐ Personal escort for the author;

☐ Ordering of books;

☐ Distribution of books and materials to teachers;

☐ Book sales and returns;

☐ Scheduling of participating classes;

☐ Class projects;

☐ Refreshments;

☐ Publicity and public relations.

Any Volunteers?

You may eventually have to assign some of these responsibilities, but in the beginning stages, it is usually better to ask for volunteers. Because of a special interest in journalism, someone will want to be in charge of publicity. Someone else may feel more comfortable in planning refreshments, and so on.

Read This Book!

Make sure every committee member reads HOW TO CAPTURE LIVE AUTHORS AND BRING THEM TO YOUR SCHOOLS from cover to cover to familiarize themselves with their particular areas and with the responsibilities of others. The better informed each member becomes, the better he or she will understand his or her function in relationship to those of everyone else. It also provides a safeguard. In the event one of your committee members becomes ill or has an emergency, it is easier for a last-minute substitute to take over.

Checklist —
One Month Before the Event

Assign people to each of the following duties:

☐ Coordinator of author travel and lodging;

☐ Coordinator of local transportation for author;

☐ Coordinator of meals for author;

☐ Author's personal escort for the day or days;

☐ Book Sales Coordinator;

☐ Refreshment Coordinator;

☐ Publicity Coordinator;

☐ Hosts for lunch and dinner (perhaps breakfast too).

Then be sure the following things are done:

☐ Arrange for the author's travel and lodging.

☐ Arrange for author's local transportation.

☐ Arrange for author's meals.

☐ The author's personal escort knows his or her responsibilities. (Discussed in detail in Chapter 10.)

☐ Develop schedules, including number of classes and students per session.

☐ Give a copy of the author's biography and bibliography to teachers and principals.

☐ Plan publicity and write news releases.

☐ Hire and/or schedule a photographer.

☐ Meet with participating teachers to discuss schedules, projects, reading of books to classes, etc.

☐ Send invitations to the superintendent, board members and sponsors.

☐ Order books to be sold if you have not already done so.

☐ Send a note to or phone the author, both as a reminder and to again inquire about his or her needs, and also to finalize travel plans and reservations.

Checklist — One Week Before the Event

Meet with all Coordinators and check to see if the following have been done:

☐ Travel and lodging arrangements are confirmed.

☐ Final lunch and dinner reservations are made.

☐ Books to sell have arrived.

☐ Reminders of the event have been sent to the superintendent, principals, board members, sponsors and parents.

☐ An updated schedule is prepared for EVERYONE.

☐ A speaker's podium, amplifier and microphone, screen and any other equipment requested by the author have been scheduled.

☐ All equipment is functioning and in proper condition.

☐ Necessary room and seating arrangements have been made with the custodians.

☐ Responsibilities and schedules have been discussed with the author's escort.

☐ Classes are finalizing their projects.

☐ The photographer has been reminded to be on time and to bring plenty of film.

Guest Authors Appreciate:

• Receiving a written confirmation and schedule well beforehand.

• Students who are familiar with at least one of the author's books (two are even better) and aware of the others.

• Students who are prepared for the author's visit.

• Books being ordered well in advance and in sufficient number.

• One host or hostess who is responsible throughout the day.

• No more than four large presentations a day.

• Payment and reimbursement made as quickly as the system allows.

— Sandy Asher, author of
TEDDY TEABURY'S
FABULOUS FACT

— William Steig,
author and illustrator of
SYLVESTER AND
THE MAGIC PEBBLE

Will You Tell Us a "Horror Story" About a Program Disaster?

No, it was *too* horrible!

— Dorothy Francis, author of CAPTAIN MORGANA MASON

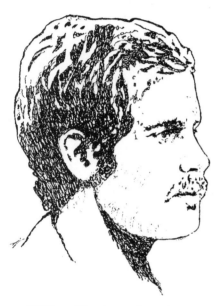

— William Sleator, author of ONCE, SAID DARLENE

A Guest Speaker's Nightmare

A school with no place to park, no map of a large building, and children "warmed up" by shouting games.

— Mary Francis Shura, author of MISTER WOLF AND ME

☐ Media news releases have been approved and the Publicity Coordinator has PERSONALLY contacted television and radio stations and newspapers.

☐ Final arrangements are made for meeting the author and for local transportation to and from the airport and to and from school.

Arrange the Author's Welcome and Offer Transportation

If your author is arriving from out of town, schedule a person to meet him or her at the airport or place of lodging. Most authors prefer to be met at the airport and driven to the hotel/motel. However, some would rather not meet new people until they have had a chance to rest and freshen up. Give your author a choice.

When Sending a Driver to the Airport

If the author is to be met at the airport, be sure the person who meets the author is **there and waiting**. Make sure the person assigned this responsibility is the most dependable of the dependable. Don't choose someone who is prone to making deadlines by the skin of the teeth or one who is habitually accustomed to showing up thirty minutes late. Also have a substitute standing by in case of a last-minute complication. There is nothing worse than to arrive at a strange airport and not be able to find the person who is to meet you.

If the Author Is Driving, Furnish Complete Directions

If your author is driving, make certain he or she receives an easy-to-read-and-follow map, along with detailed instructions, of how to locate the hotel/motel and the school. Keep directions as simple as possible. Don't include complicated shortcut routes, but provide those which are most clearly indicated with street signs and prominent landmarks. Leave nothing to chance. Before you send the map, test it out by driving the route yourself.

Numbers, Please!

An extra precautionary measure is to provide your visitor with the home and office telephone numbers of:

The school;

The Program Coordinator;

The person in charge of the author's local transportation; and

The reserved hotel/motel.

Final Updates

Whether or not there have been changes in the schedule, upon the author's arrival, be sure to give him or her a fresh copy. And again, review with the author about equipment needed.

Most authors do not expect or desire to be pampered, but they do appreciate common courtesies. If, through your thoughtfulness, you make authors feel welcome and comfortable, they will not only respond favorably, but most often, they will offer their very best.

Don't Hang by Your Fingernails!

**How do we make sure
our author arrives early enough?**

Unless you enjoy hanging by your fingernails, if your author is scheduled for a full day, you have every right to insist that he or she arrives by the evening before.

If the author can't arrive until the very last minute, then you either take your chances or get another author.

Special Considerations

**Are there any special things we might do
to make the author feel more welcome?**

When traveling, little things do mean a lot. The thoughtfulness of a floral bouquet or basket of fruit placed in the hotel/motel room is really appreciated.

**If the author arrives the day before the program,
should we plan to take him or her to dinner?**

If the author arrives early enough the evening before, you or one of your committee members may wish to take your guest to dinner or plan a small dinner for a group of no more than eight people. Many authors enjoy a time to become acquainted with some of the teachers whose classes they'll be seeing the following days. However, in order to have time to rest and prepare for the next day, some would rather have a quiet meal alone or with only one person.

As host, you should find out what the author prefers before planning a party.

Do authors enjoy a tour of the area?

I do. No matter how big or small communities may be, they are always fascinating. Most authors are inquisitive and, if time allows, they may enjoy seeing the sights.

Follow the Leader!

**If the author has a car,
should we offer transportation to and from school?**

Yes. If the author agrees, make sure your driver is on time! Even if the author insists on driving his or her own car, offer to send someone to lead the way. Be sure enough time for travel is allowed in spite of morning or evening traffic. Since you've spent so much energy on programming and coordinating the event, you don't want to lose the author on the day of the program or learn that he or she is delayed by a traffic jam.

A Genuine Interest

When I'm in new territory, I especially enjoy a tour of the area for an hour or so on one afternoon after the work is finished. It need not be a grand tour. Indeed, if there are noted attractions, I should make my own arrangements to stay an extra period of time to see them. Also, after a busy day of book talks, serious museum-going does not appeal to me. But a ride through a town, no matter its size, and a look at some of its buildings, parks, or whatever is always interesting.

I return home then with the satisfaction of having met youngsters who are reading and adults who are encouraging them to do so, and I have had a better glimpse of their neighborhood, as it were, than the ride from the airport to the motel would have provided.

— Robert Burch, author of
IDA EARLY COMES
OVER THE MOUNTAIN

Drivers and Escorts
Really Appreciated

The aspect of hospitality I feel is most important is a morning pick-up to take me to the schools, as they are sometimes hard to locate. A guide or hostess to show me from room to room is also most helpful.

— Ida Chittum, author of
TALES OF TERROR

A Matter of Interest

The person picking up the speaker at the motel should not pump the speaker with questions — particularly if the drive takes longer than ten minutes, causing the voice and the enthusiasm to wane before ever arriving at school. I appreciate the person's conversation about the character of the school and items of interest about it, or hearing about the person's interests in the book world. I like to know what's currently going on in the schools.

— Mary Calhoun, author of
    the KATIE JOHN series

— Norma Klein, author of
    MOM, THE WOLFMAN, AND ME

Checklist —
One Day Before the Event

Check and double-check **everything**:

☐ Review travel arrangements.

☐ Review hotel/motel reservations.

☐ Be sure the author's transportation is coordinated and will be ready and on time.

☐ Review meal arrangements.

☐ Be sure the author's personal escort knows what to do and that introductions are properly prepared and ready.

☐ Be sure plans are set to provide water and a glass for the speaker during each session.

☐ Be sure a supply of pens are on hand for autographing books.

☐ Meet with teachers to review the final schedule.

☐ Make sure everyone understands that sessions are to begin and end promptly.

☐ Make sure all classroom projects are properly displayed and the "Welcome" banners are hung.

☐ Approve room and seating arrangements for the sessions.

☐ Make sure custodians understand their responsibilities and are prepared for any alterations.

☐ Make sure coffee and refreshments will be ready.

☐ Be sure your Publicity Coordinator again PERSONALLY contacts television and radio stations and newspapers.

☐ Be sure there are sufficient numbers of people to assist your Book Sales Coordinator in handling sales and that the tables are properly arranged.

☐ Be sure teachers have had students print their names NEATLY in copies of books to be autographed.

☐ Remind the superintendent, principals, board members, sponsors, parents and other invited guests of the event.

☐ Be sure the photographer will be on time and bring plenty of film.

☐ And be sure to check all audio/visual equipment to make sure it is properly set up, in good condition, and functioning. Check the microphone and amplifier, the slide projector and overhead projector, and make sure the screen is in first-class condition.

The Mouse That Couldn't Roar

Since I am also an illustrator and usually show slides of my work to students, I am particularly sensitive about program coordinators double-checking equipment. I learned long ago not to rely on school equipment. After turning on a number of inoperable projectors that kept changing slides rapid-fire whether I wanted them changed or not, I became convinced to carry my own.

If screens weren't so large, I'd carry my own screen too. I have faced school screens that are torn and patched, and some have had words of questionable taste scrawled across their fronts.

In one classroom, when the teacher raised the screen, half of the children yelled: "Oh, gross!" and feigned sounds of throwing up. There, squashed on the surface, were the remains of a dead mouse. Judging from the state of decomposition, the unfortunate creature was not a recent casualty, but had probably been rolled inside several months before.

With much interest, we watched as the maintenance man removed the remains and tried to wash off the stain. I have no doubt it was the high point of the day. And it was the first and only time I have ever been upstaged by a dead mouse.

So — open the screen!

Operate the projectors!

Speak into the microphone!

Leave nothing to chance!

After you have checked every item and feel confident that everyone and everything is present and accounted for, then try if you will to get a good night's sleep.

An Absolute Delight!

Since I'm frequently asked to speak about, perform and/or write poetry with classes, the "perfect engagement" was one where the teacher had thoroughly prepared her class for my visit. They knew my favorite poets, a couple of my poems, and the approach I used. There were also posters in the room that featured quotes from my book. In addition, the students were prepared to ask intelligent questions about poets and poetry. The day was an absolute delight, with the students and I learning together.

— Greg Denman, author of
WHEN YOU'VE MADE IT YOUR OWN
— Teaching Poetry to Young People

A Texas "Howdy" and Southern Comfort!

Twice I've been invited to the Dallas area — Arlington, Irving, etc., for four to five days in the schools. Mary Lankford and others have several authors or illustrators in each year and have the model program for presenting them. There, it isn't a matter of "every child in the school must see the author," for over the years, each kid gets a chance.

I was scheduled to speak to certain grades, two programs in the morning, two in the afternoon. The children were well prepared to know and be interested in my work. Tons of my books were sold, and I autographed them in the evening at my comfortable motel.

There was pleasant hospitality. Special dinners were wonderful — with delicious food and stimulating shoptalk. Lunches were at delightful restaurants, and although we stayed on schedule, I didn't feel rushed.

— Mary Calhoun, author of
   the KATIE JOHN series

Robert C. Lee

10

READY OR NOT, THE BIG DAY ARRIVES

Top Priorities — Start on Time!   End on Time!

The author's books are read. The students and teachers are ready. The schedules are posted. The banners are hung. And the class projects are completed (well, almost). Don't forget to pick up the author!

Now is the time when all your planning, all your meetings, and all your telephone calls pay off. Other than the author fainting in the hallway or coming down with laryngitis, if anything goes wrong, except for you and your committee members, no one else will know — they'll think you planned it that way.

Two things are of prime importance:

1. Start every session on time.

2. End every session on time.

If your committee makes the time schedule work, everything else usually falls into place.

Stay Three Steps Ahead!

You and your committee members should always be three steps ahead of everyone else at all times. If that means you have to get up three hours earlier, then do so. Get to the school and make double-sure that:

- The rooms are properly prepared.

- Chairs are arranged.

- All equipment is in place and in proper working order.

- Coffee is made.

- A glass and water are provided for your speaker.

- And most importantly — **make sure the first session starts precisely on time.**

— Cena Christopher Draper, author of
RIM OF THE RIDGE

Advice to Visiting Authors

Never speak longer than you have promised...or less. Adhere to your time schedule strictly — no more, no less.

— Ida Chittum, author of
TALES OF TERROR

Stop the Clock!

I do not prepare a speech. I ask the organizers what subject I should talk about and how long they wish me to talk. They tell me and I try to comply.

I was invited to a Book Conference in New York, mostly attended by librarians, along with an older, very well known children's author and artist and an author who had made an excellent film for children. We were asked to speak for 20 minutes. The first author took out a manuscript and read for one hour. Then the film-maker spoke for his 20 minutes. I was last and people were leaving — it was after 11:00 p.m.

I had been asked to talk on how I had illustrated the Laura Ingalls Wilder books. "That is fully written in the HORN BOOK of that year," I said, and allowed all to catch the last train home.

Several years ago in Kansas, I was asked to speak for about 40 minutes. When I went beyond that time, a notice was placed before me on the desk, saying, "PLEASE STOP". Touché.

— Garth Williams, illustrator of
Laura Ingalls Wilder's
LITTLE HOUSE books

Move 'Em In!

If students must move from their classroom into a multipurpose room or another room, make certain that they start soon enough to be in the assigned room and settled at least **five minutes** before the first session is scheduled to begin. If you know of teachers who have trouble getting their acts together and rarely get their classes anywhere on time, go to their rooms early enough to prod them down the hall.

You do not want the author to have to stand around and wait for the group to assemble.

If you allow the first session to start late, you'll either have to shorten that time period or play "catch up" all day.

As the first session gets under way, members of the committee should be concentrating on preparations for the next session or activity.

The Importance of Providing the Best Escort for Your Visiting Author

Other than a good program coordinator and an efficient organizing committee for your author-related program, the most important job is that of the author's personal escort. A good escort's functions, are:

- To make sure the author is in the proper place at the right time.

- To make sure each session begins on time.

- To properly introduce the author to teachers, principals, students and visitors.

- To properly introduce the author to assembled groups.

- To make sure the author has a supply of pens for autographing books.

- To make sure the teacher (or assigned person) in each session has provided the author with a glass and water.

- To give the author a prearranged signal **five minutes** before it is time to begin the question and answer period.

- To make sure the question and answer period begins on time.

- To give the author a prearranged signal when **five minutes** remain in the session.

- To diplomatically end the session on time, even if the author is still talking.

- To guide the author to the room assigned for breaks and make certain he or she has the opportunity to rest without being barraged by over-zealous fans.

Select Author's Escort with Extreme Care

The author's escort should be an extremely responsible and responsive person. Do not assign anyone to this job just because he or she has nothing else to do. Next to the author, there will be no one who will work harder — it is a full-time job.

**Should we assign one escort for a full day
or different ones for each session?**

If at all possible, assign **one escort** for the full day or days. Remember, the author is in new surroundings, meeting new people at every turn. One dependable escort can really be a stabilizing factor.

How long should a proper introduction be?

A proper introduction of the author is **short**, informative, **short**, friendly, **short** and to the point.

"And here she is,...!" is too short.

The following is an example of a good introduction:

> Our guest author has written ten books, among them are *Title 1*, *Title 2*, and *Title 3*. She is the recipient of the Newbery Award and the Children's Literature Award. She makes her home in Boston, Massachusetts, and has come here today to tell you about her work. It is my privilege to introduce Janice Longfellow Shakespeare.

Anything longer cuts into the time the author has with the students. Anything shorter is usually off-the-cuff and not worth saying.

**Should the escort stay in the room
during every presentation?**

Absolutely! So he or she must be someone who is willing to hear a similar presentation three or four times and still show enthusiasm, or at least appear to be interested and alert.

A good escort has no time to become bored, because he or she is constantly evaluating the situation to anticipate the needs of the author and to monitor the easy flow of activities.

Are there any supplies the escort should have?

Yes. Pencil and paper to make notes and a supply of pens for the author to use in autographing books. And above all, an accurate wristwatch. In some schools, no two clocks indicate the same time.

The Best Author Escort
Is Always There — Really There!

The escort should make sure every session begins on time. If one group is late in arriving, the time should be deducted from that session instead of penalizing other groups.

I have had wonderful, efficient escorts; others have needed full-time keepers themselves.

The best escorts are always there — *really there*!

As we prepare for the next session, a good escort will tell me something about each of the teachers — their favorite projects, special interests, and hobbies — which really helps in making meaningful conversation.

Every time I meet a new person, a competent escort will say the person's name clearly, and tell me what grade he or she teaches, or if the person is a coordinator, an administrator or a parent volunteer.

A capable escort not only leads the author into conversations with

— Martha Bennett Stiles, author of
ONE AMONG THE INDIANS

Proper Behavior

While an author is speaking to students, I don't understand why some teachers will sit in a conspicuous place, ostentatiously grading papers or reading books they have picked from the library shelves, as if nothing I say could possibly interest them.

I also don't like for teachers to play "sergeant-major-general" while I'm speaking to students. In one school, the teachers jabbed the sixth graders with pointed fingers every time they budged. Needless to say, the students fulfilled their teachers' expectations and behaved like savages, until I asked that the teachers trust me and the kids and leave the discipline up to us. The students then became relaxed and behaved very well.

— Jane Resh Thomas, author of
THE PRINCESS IN THE PIGPEN

And the Machines Grumbled On

I've fortunately just one horror story. It occurred as my second experience in presenting a program; the first had gone so excitingly I was no way prepared for the bad that could happen.

That program was set up in a bare, echoing room-of-all purposes that included three pop-dispensing machines crowded against one wall and frequently grumbling at each other to move over. The audience came in: grades one through eight, with no differentiation or any evident preparation. All of the teachers retired to a smoking room, save one left on monitor duty, which she seemed to think meant sitting quietly and taking copious notes on misbehavior.

When I tried to phrase a statement for one age group, the age groups on hold got understandable restless. Finally some young kids went over to investigate the noises coming from the machines. Before long I was there too because it seemed the interesting thing to do. It became surreal. Now I would achieve order some way or leave, but then I kept on till the bell, and the machines grumbled just as much when I left as when I came.

— Peter Zachary Cohen, author of DEADLY GAME AT STONY CREEK

Sound Advice

Gatherings in hard-floored, ratty gymnasiums should be avoided. I hate speaking in hallway libraries where classes are passing through.

— Mary Calhoun, author of the KATIE JOHN series

people, but knows how to graciously conclude conversations when necessary.

I cannot emphasize too much just how important the escort is to the success of the program. Finding the best person for this job should be a prime consideration. Once you do, be sure the escort completely understands the responsibilities and functions of the position.

May we videotape the author's sessions?

Some authors will readily approve videotaping of sessions. But consult the author **in advance**, because some feel the presence of a camera is disruptive and others are extremely camera-shy.

Attention, Please!

What if the students become fidgety during the author's presentation?

Students become restless for a variety of reasons:
- **The classes haven't been properly prepared;**
- **The author's subject isn't compatible with the age group;**
- **The author isn't a good speaker;**
- **The students are not physically comfortable;**
- **The program coincides with an unusual occurrence; or**
- **Changes in the weather are imminent.**

When the Classes Are Not Properly Prepared

We have already discussed preparation of students for an author's visit in detail in Chapters 7 and 8.

When the Subject Matter Isn't Compatible with the Age Group

If the speaker's topic is not really interesting to students of a particular age group, you have not matched the right author with the right classes.

When an Author Is Not a Good Speaker

If you happen to get an author who cannot command the attention of his or her audience, the students, no matter what age, will become bored and restless. When this happens, a skillful escort or program coordinator will diplomatically see that the session does not run one minute over schedule or may even find a way to bring an early conclusion.

If the speaker is not charismatic, you may blame only those who recommended the author or yourselves for not getting a recommendation.

When Students Are Physically Uncomfortable

If students are physically uncomfortable, it usually isn't because of lack of facilities, but more often is due to the lack of consideration. If we adults were lined up and marched into a room, made to sit on a hard floor for forty or fifty minutes, and told to keep our hands to ourselves, we would complain to high Heaven. And rightfully so!

Anyone who concludes that sitting on the floor or crowded two-to-a-chair is uncomfortable for adults, but perfectly acceptable for children, is obviously an adult and one who has little respect for children. Although we say we love children and talk about our respect for them, we turn around and do the darnedest things to them.

I make no bones about it — I do not like to speak to children who have been herded into a room and made to sit on the floor. No matter what age, sitting on the floor is uncomfortable — even when playing jacks or shooting marbles.

If we want students to pay attention to the speaker and be on their best behavior, no matter where they are assembled — a gymnasium, an all-purpose room, or a classroom — we should make the necessary arrangements for them to be **comfortably seated**.

Students also respond to **diet**, **temperature** of the room and **time** commitments.

Immediately after lunch, hyperactivity increases and long-term attention is diminished. Food that is not easily digested can also add to the students' restlessness.

The temperature of a room may be too warm as a result of too little ventilation or overcrowding from an oversized group. Remember, even though it may be cold outside, students' bodies function as furnaces and most air return systems in classrooms aren't equipped to accommodate larger groups. You may need to set up fans or open windows.

And regardless of how famous or how good a speaker the author may be, during the last session of the day, students can become nervous about time because they are preoccupied with missing their busses.

Payment Due

I like to be paid as soon as the engagement is over. It is also disagreeable to have to wait three months to be reimbursed — not only for travel expenses, but for books I was asked to supply for sale because the school failed to have books on hand.

— Helen R. Sattler, author of
NATURE'S WEATHER
FORECASTERS

When the Program Coincides with an Unusual Occurrence

In spite of how well a program is planned, events of the day or the community can affect the proceedings.

Surely any speaker's program would have been affected the day President Kennedy was assassinated or following the explosion of the space shuttle, *Challenger*.

While I was presenting a school program several years ago, word was received that one of the students had been killed in a car accident. Although the students were extremely courteous during every session, one could sense their concern and feeling of loss.

The class in which the boy had been a member was scheduled for the last session. During questions and answers, one little boy asked if I had heard about the death of their classmate. I said I had.

Then, one by one, they began to tell me about the boy and expressed their feelings. There were tears in many eyes. There was little talk or thought about writing and illustrating books. Our time together became a quiet conversation about their classmate. I was no longer a visiting author. I was a friend. It was my privilege to have been accepted to share such a personal moment in their lives.

Authors Should Not Be Asked To Sign Bits of Paper

Teachers should announce ahead of time that the writer will not be signing bits of paper, for I think time used to sign the papers of a whole class is a waste of time for all concerned. I feel that books only, for a child or for the school library, should be signed.

— Marian Potter, author of
BLATHERSKITE

Organizing Autograph Sessions

Autographing can sometimes be a problem if children are allowed to get autographs on scraps of paper, especially when time is short. Usually I talk this over ahead of time with the teacher in charge, and she will tell the children "Autographs only if you have a copy of one of Ms. Hall's books." And then it helps if there are teachers standing by to see that the children line up in some sort of order rather than crowding around, jostling the table I'm writing on.

— Lynn Hall, author of
  THE LEAVING

Something for Everyone

To give or not to give autographs? This question is difficult to decide.

A visiting author does not have the time to give autographs to every single child. Yet it seems unfair to allow autographs only for those who can afford to BUY a book. Children can be hurt this way and I have even seen tears.

In my case, a happy solution to the problem of autographs involves a poem I wrote and sold to *The New York Catalog for Kids*. When the magazine published it, it was illustrated with birds. I autograph this poem, the teachers make copies, and every child is given one and can even color the picture if they wish.

This pleases everyone and each child has a memento of the BIG DAY!

— Ida Chittum, author of
  TALES OF TERROR

Best Wishes

If autographing books is to happen at a school, *enough time* should be allowed for it, and it should not be during the author's program or rest periods.

— Mary Calhoun, author of
  the KATIE JOHN series

When Changes in the Weather Are Imminent

Anyone who spends much time observing students soon realizes, or at least begins to suspect, that young people are terrific barometers. They respond individually and collectively to atmospheric conditions.

Best Wishes and Fondest Regards

When should authors autograph their books?

Some authors prefer to have their books stacked on a table, removed from interruptions, so they can sign autographs in a relaxed atmosphere. Others choose to be even more remote and sign books in the privacy of their rooms during the evening.

However, others, myself included, would rather autograph books at the close of every session in order to have the opportunity to speak briefly with each student on a one-to-one basis.

A word of caution: When authors autograph books at the close of sessions, that time should be considered as part of the session, not the author's break time.

It is also an enormous help if students NEATLY PRINT their names inside the books to be autographed. This way, the author can easily see the correct spelling of names. Considering how many inventive ways parents have found to spell even the simplest names — "Debby, Debbie, Debi, Debee," and so on, authors appreciate all the help they get.

Students can also become so shy and tongue-tied that when their mouths move, little or no sound comes out. Some become so nervous they even misspell their own names.

Should authors be expected to sign pieces of paper?

Although most authors are happy to sign autographs for students, it should be understood that there are limits to how many times the same hand can scrawl the same signature at one sitting — *especially when hastily scribbled on the torn-off corner of a sheet of notebook paper, a paper sack, or a wrinkled sheet retrieved from a wastepaper basket.*

Besides winding up with writer's cramp, if the author sits and signs his or her name for long periods of time, more productive activities and instruction with students and teachers are sacrificed.

A good rule to set and maintain in regard to autographing, is: The author will autograph **books** and **books only**.

So that every student has an opportunity to have a memento of the day, some inventive teachers and librarians have four bookmarkers drawn out on one 8 1/2-inch by 11-inch sheet of paper and ask the author to sign all four. During the day, the sheets are Xeroxed and copies are cut into strips so that each student receives one bookmark.

Where should we set up a table for book sales?

Not next to the author, please. And never expect the author to handle any of the money. Although most authors appreciate their books being sold, they do not like being placed in a position where it appears that they are involved with the sales.

If you have set up an autographing table for the author in the same room as the sales table, make sure the tables are placed a considerable distance from each other.

A number of authors, myself included, would rather not even be in the same room where sales are taking place.

In some schools, the librarian is in charge of ordering, selling and returning books. However, he or she must not be expected to handle everything alone. Be sure that assistance is available from teachers, students and/or parent volunteers.

Promptly and Discreetly!

When should we pay the author?

It is customary for the author to be given a check for his or her fee immediately following the event. The words any experienced speaker hates to hear, are: "Send us a bill" or "I'll turn in a requisition to the main office." The author knows that payment may take months.

Since you have agreed in advance to the amount of the author's fee, have the check prepared prior to the visit. If you require an itemized list of expenses or if the expenses must be presented in any special form, be sure to advise the author. Take responsibility to see that payment is issued **promptly**, instead of allowing the bill to gather dust at the head office where checks are written only on the third Thursday, every two months.

Also, **discreetly** present the check for the fee to the author, and give it at a time when he or she can conveniently place it in a billfold or briefcase for safekeeping. Don't just hand over payment during the activities.

In short — please pay the author **promptly** and **discreetly**.

The Last Session
Doesn't End the Day

The mark of a good host is not only determined by how well the author is greeted and treated before and during the course of an engagement, but by the consideration he or she receives after the sessions have ended.

Hosts who really appreciate the efforts of the author will continue to care about the comfort of their visitor even after the last speech has been spoken and the last question has been answered.

Don't Forget the Author

To properly wrap up the visit, provide personnel to help the author pack equipment, carry it to the nearest exit, and load it in the car. To assure that these needs are being properly met, either you or the author's escort should stay until everything is packed and loaded. Don't assume that maintenance people will provide such assistance — sometimes they have a way of disappearing, even if the task has been specifically assigned to them.

Front and Center!

When the day's activities are concluded, be sure to provide transpor-

The Seven-Foot Cowboy
and the Wad of Cash

I have been handed payment at the most unexpected times — while walking down a hallway between sessions, while autographing books, and even while speaking to an audience.

My strangest time of payment, however, was during an evening function which concluded a week of programs. My visit had been sponsored by a regional rodeo. After being introduced, I started toward the podium. Suddenly a seven-foot cowboy stood up, met me on the stage, and handed me more than fifteen hundred dollars in bills, none larger than twenties.

Well, the money was rolled into a wad that would have choked a horse. I was momentarily tempted to walk straight out the door and make a quick getaway. And I might have done just that if I hadn't noticed the size of the shoulders on the seven-foot cowboy.

During the first five minutes of my speech, I kept searching for a pocket in my suit that was big enough to accommodate the roll of bills. I finally stacked the money on a shelf beneath the podium and promptly forgot about it. Two hours later, I happened to remember the money. The program coordinator immediately drove back to the school, and believe it or not, someone had taken the cash from the shelf and left it in full view on top of the podium.

— David Melton, author of
WRITTEN & ILLUSTRATED BY...

tation to take the author back to the hotel/motel.

Whether the author wishes to return home that evening or the following day, also arrange for transportation to the airport.

If the author has come to speak to classes for two or more days, whatever evening plans you make should be scheduled after consultation with the author. Most authors know their own energy levels and state of health. Some prefer a quiet dinner and rest. Others are **up, up, up** and ready to **go, go, go** for whatever you have planned for the evening.

If a dinner party is planned, be sure to keep the numbers of people small. Remember, the author has expended a great amount of energy in speaking to and meeting new people the whole day.

"Hope You Make Your Flight!"

When taking the author to the airport, don't just drop your visitor at the door like a "hot potato." Be sure the driver helps with the luggage and offers the courtesy of staying, not only until boarding time, but until the plane is airborne. Don't leave the author alone to discover that a flight has been delayed by hours or canceled.

You should plan for the author's departure with thoughtful care and cordiality.

Beyond the Call of Duty

On the side of the angels — I once went to the wrong city, thereby requiring someone to drive two hours instead of ten minutes to get me (and, of course, two hours back). This person arrived with smiles, good cheer, and a warm, enthusiastic welcome, instead of boiling oil and pointed sticks.

— Barbara Robinson, author of
THE BEST CHRISTMAS
PAGEANT EVER

Don't Leave
Your Guest in the Lurch

Since I use audio/visual equipment and travel with a caravan of boxes and cases, I am more than sensitive on the issue of the final wrap-up of a program. I have been left stranded to pack and carry by myself at some of the most undeserving times.

Several years ago, I was engaged to spend five days in one school system. The public librarian phoned me and asked if I would consider doing an evening presentation of my audio/visual show on Harry S. Truman which I had designed for the Truman Library.

"Of course, we have no money, but the people of our community would really appreciate it," she quickly assured me.

I agreed to show the program without charge.

That night, despite a heavy thunderstorm, the library had more people than chairs, so the program had to be shown twice, extending the occasion longer than had been originally planned. Both audiences were most

receptive and many stayed afterwards to enjoy refreshments and congenial conversations.

As the last people departed, I began to dismantle my equipment, which took a considerable amount of time since it involved a multiprojector phase dissolve unit.

The librarian, who had been very friendly up to this point, suddenly walked over to me and asked how long the packing would take. When I said thirty or forty minutes, she acted as if I was to blame for the two showings and late hour, and she announced flatly that I would have to pack the next morning because she was tired and was ready to go home.

Since I was scheduled for a full day of school programs the following day, I told her I had no choice but to pack that evening, and I continued boxing the equipment.

Instead of offering to help, she stormed into her office, where I could overhear her complaining to her assistant behind the closed door. When

I began carrying the equipment to the car, neither she nor her assistant offered any help. When the last box was loaded, she locked the doors of the library and without so much as a "thank-you" or a "kiss my foot," she climbed into her car and peeled rubber all the way out of the parking lot.

Last year I was scheduled to return to that community to speak to the regional council of the International Reading Association. About a month prior to my visit, my secretary received a phone call from that same public librarian.

"Tell her I am not available."

"But, shouldn't I find out what she wants?" my secretary asked.

"No," I replied, "I'm not available for *anything* she wants."

— David Melton, author of
WRITTEN & ILLUSTRATED
BY...

N. M. Bodecker

11

THE FINAL WRAP-UP FOR A NEW BEGINNING

Onward and Upward!

The day following an author-related school program is like the day after Christmas — the excitement has been shared, the adrenalin has flowed, the fun has been had, the party is over. Now someone has to pick up the empty cups and paper plates and move back into the everyday world.

Do It Now!
— Do It Right!

Remember, for every high there is an equivalent low. Although it's easy to put off or lay aside the necessary steps of wrapping up your school program, you and your committee members would be well advised to muster your energies and complete the finishing touches as quickly as possible. It is much easier to secure assistance while the enthusiasm still hangs in the air.

Although some people consider the packing up of return books and the writing of thank-you notes to be the final phase of a program, I don't. I look upon these activities as the **beginning** of next year's bigger and even better program. If you and your committee touch every base, thank every sponsor, and get enthusiastic evaluations from teachers, students, principals, board members and parents, you can expect to receive even more cooperation and support the following year.

So take the time to wrap up everything in the right way!

— Ouida Sebestyen, author of
WORDS BY HEART

Checklist for Wrap-up Activities

☐ Write thank-you notes to all sponsors and contributing supporters. Don't forget all school personnel, including custodians.

Fair To Expect

One hopes to find respect for the authors, even if they aren't big names.

At Central Missouri State University, Phil Sadler and his staff prepare so carefully and accommodate authors so thoughtfully. A variety of events is scheduled to acquaint us with other writers and to meet a number of faculty members and librarians. At the same time, the writer's privacy is respected, and we aren't forced into more togetherness than we want.

Bottom line: There, the writer is made to feel like a visiting V.I.P. and thus is willing to put in a long day of talking to one class after another.

— Thomas Millstead, author of
  CAVE OF THE
  MOVING SHADOWS

— T. Ernesto Bethancourt, author of
  the DORIS FEIN mystery series

☐ Ask teachers and students to also write thank-you notes to sponsors. Business people can't help but be charmed when they receive a package of thank-you letters from students.

☐ As soon as possible, get prints of pictures. Then assemble a **complete**, and **I mean complete**, scrapbook of everything connected with the author's visit, including evaluations, comments, news articles, bulletins, and letters to and from parents. **This scrapbook will prove of great benefit in obtaining funds and other assistance for next year's event**.

☐ If you have received nice verbal comments during or following the program, ask the persons to write down their statements so you can include these in your scrapbook.

☐ Also create an exciting and attractive collage of pictures and articles on the bulletin board in the main hallway for everyone to enjoy. The collage also serves as a reminder that your program achieved success.

☐ If there are any unsold books to return to the publishers, do so immediately. The chief complaint of publishers about school programs is that too often books are not returned for months. Don't let that happen.

☐ Prepare a memorandum to the administration and faculty. Just as it was your job to let everyone know of the event before it happened, now let everyone know what a rip-roaring success it was!

☐ To keep their attention even longer, have teachers and students begin to make lists of authors they would like to meet the following school year.

Evaluating the Success of Your Author-Related Program?

You can assess the organization.

You can appraise the quality of the author's presentation.

You can certainly tell if the students and teachers enjoyed the author's visit.

But beyond those three observations, you probably can't evaluate the full measure of your program's success.

If you look at the teachers the following day, they're teaching. But due to the author's visit, perhaps the quality of their teaching and their appreciation of books have been significantly improved.

Look at the students. They're back in class, working on new projects. But because they've met a live author, perhaps the quality of their learning, their creative abilities, and their eagerness to read more and better books have been accelerated.

Even if you take a closer look, you may not be able to see the dynamic changes that have taken place.. But somewhere within one, maybe two, or all of the classes there are students who now dare to dream that someday they, too, might write books and be asked to speak to students.

Look as you may, unless you have exceptional psychic powers, you won't be able to recognize those who have been changed so dramatically. Their changes do not show on the surface, but are ignited somewhere within the regions where dreams begin.

I have no doubt that on the day I met A. B. Guthrie, Jr., my life was altered. I'm sure my father didn't notice it that late afternoon and my teacher didn't see it the following morning. The possibilities I sensed within didn't make me any taller, or any heavier, or transform my features in any way, but I was changed nevertheless.

Why do we plan author-related programs? For the same reasons we teach students — not only because we appreciate what wonders they truly are, but because we want to exert positive influences in the types of adults they may become and hope to enhance the quality of their lives.

The day an author speaks to your students should be a very special day when moments are captured and dreams are born.

The author's visit occurred because you and your committee members provided such a wonderful opportunity.

Next month's programs and next year's programs are being planned because people like you sincerely care about students and realize the importance of encouraging joyful experiences in reading and creative writing.

So set your traps and bait your hooks! It's time to capture live authors and bring them to your school!

In your quest, I wish you every success and hope that the information within this book will prove most beneficial.

— David Melton

The Heart Is Willing, But Time Doesn't Permit

Often classes will follow-up an author's visit with thank-you letters and their pictures. However, because some children have great enthusiasm, teachers should gently help them to realize that most authors don't have time to reply to each child. I would be sorry for a child to feel let down because further questions or requests were not answered. At most, *one* reply to the whole class is what should be expected.

— Mary Calhoun, author of
the KATIE JOHN series

David Melton —author and illustrator

David Melton is one of the most versatile and prolific talents on the literary and art scenes today. His literary works span the gamut of factual prose, analytical essays, newsreporting, magazine articles, features, short stories, poetry and novels in both the adult and juvenile fields. When reviewing his credits, it is difficult to believe that such an outpouring of creative efforts came from just one person. In seventeen years, twenty-four of his books have been published, several of which have been translated into a number of languages.

Mr. Melton has illustrated ten of his own books and three by other authors, while many of his drawings and paintings have been reproduced as fine art prints, posters, puzzles, calendars, book jackets, record covers, mobiles and note cards, and they have been featured in national publications.

Mr. Melton has also gained wide reputation as a guest speaker and teacher. He has spoken to hundreds of professional, social and civic groups, relating the problems that confront parents and teachers of learning-disabled and handicapped children, and he has influenced the mandates of change in the field of special education and therapies for brain-injured children. He is also a frequent guest on local and national radio and television talk shows.

Since a number of Mr. Melton's books are enjoyed by children, he has visited hundreds of schools nationwide as a principal speaker in Author-in-Residence Programs, Young Authors' Days, and Children's Literature Festivals. He also conducts in-service seminars for teachers and teaches professional writing courses throughout the country.

To encourage and celebrate the creativity of students, Mr. Melton has developed the highly acclaimed teacher's manual, WRITTEN & ILLUSTRATED BY..., which is used in thousands of schools in teaching students to write and illustrate original books by *THE MELTON METHOD*. To provide opportunities for students to become professionally published authors and illustrators, in association with Landmark Editions, Inc., he helped initiate THE NATIONAL WRITTEN & ILLUSTRATED BY... AWARDS CONTEST FOR STUDENTS.

WRITTEN & ILLUSTRATED BY...
Critically Acclaimed
by Reviewers and Classroom Teachers

WRITTEN & ILLUSTRATED BY... is an exceptional book! It provides step-by-step instructions for helping any teacher to involve his or her students in the various aspects of writing and producing books. David Melton is thorough in his topics that range from contracting for a product to the use of space in a layout. **This is a book built from practical experience. Just browsing through it stimulates excitement for writing!**

> — Joyce E. Juntune, Executive Director
> National Association for Gifted Children

...In lively, easy-to-follow lesson plans, Mr. Melton guides teachers in a precise, step-by-step process that skillfully assigns the appropriate tasks to and balances the activities of the "academic" brain and the "creative" brain.

The results are dazzling!

For every elementary school teacher and for teachers of English, composition, and creative writing, **here is a book-companion that will renew your excitement and commitment to the art of teaching** and to the children entrusted to your care, and will give you a sure-fire project guaranteed to please parents, principals, fellow teachers, and, most of all, your students.

> — Children's Book Review Service, Inc.

WRITTEN & ILLUSTRATED BY... encourages students to use both the "academic" and "creative" brains as a means of exploring and developing novel aspects of learning. **...the author is to be commended for developing a work which guides creative thinking into several new directions.** The book should prove to be very useful in supplementing the standard language arts curriculum.

> — CURRICULUM REVIEW
> Jack V. Powell, Associate Professor
> Department of Elementary Education
> University of Georgia, Athens

The Melton Method of utilizing both the academic and the creative brains of students in their development of books is so innovative it sets the mind racing. Seeing is believing — My students' writing and artistic skills improved immediately and the excitement students gained in their own creative efforts was electric. **This is one of the most positive approaches to teaching I've ever experienced.**

> — Jean Tucker, Journalism and English Instructor
> Allen County Community College
> Iola, Kansas

Written & Illustrated by...

a revolutionary two-brain approach for teaching students how to write and illustrate amazing books

David Melton

ISBN 0-933849-00-1   softcover

WRITTEN & ILLUSTRATED BY... **is definitely on target for school objectives in basic communication skills.**...By creating an end product, the process of writing and illustrating books does for language arts what a science fair does for science curriculum.

> — Marge Hagerty, Library Media Specialist
> Chinn Elementary School
> Park Hill District
> Kansas City, Missouri

WRITTEN & ILLUSTRATED BY... has become my "bible" for preparing my language arts students for Young Author Conferences.

If you want a "how-to" book that really works — this is it!

> — Judy O'Brien, teacher
> Patrick Hamilton Middle School
> Dowagiac, Michigan

THE NATIONAL WRITTEN & ILLUSTRATED BY... AWARDS CONTEST FOR STUDENTS

by Marge Hagerty
School Library Media Specialist

Books for students, written and illustrated by students! What a wonderful idea! Our school has all of the Landmark series in our library, but these books are seldom on the shelf. My students are fascinated with the books, and so am I. The book subjects are varied and popular, the illustrations are superb and eye catching, and the reading levels are suited to the subjects.

More than that, each book presents an invitation to students to write and illustrate books of their own. My students like to read about the authors and imagine what it would be like to be published themselves. No better motivation can be found for inspiring students to write and draw creatively or in fact for encouraging them to read.

The CONTEST offers exciting publishing opportunities to students. Each year three winning students' books are published by Landmark. The student winners are offered publishing contracts, are paid royalties on book sales, and receive all-expense-paid trips to Landmark's offices in Kansas City, Missouri. While there, the young author/illustrators have a private office where professional editors and art directors assist them edit their manuscripts and show them how to develop final illustrations.

One of the high points of the trip is the opportunity for students to work with Landmark's Creative Coordinator, David Melton, the author/illustrator of 30 books and the initiator of the CONTEST. In working with young people, Mr. Melton skillfully brings out the very best talent in each student.

The CONTEST has ignited the interest of hundreds of thousands of students. Through hands-on experience, they are learning valuable information about book development and format.

Landmark Receives National Honor

The NATIONAL WRITTEN & ILLUSTRATED BY...AWARDS CONTEST FOR STUDENTS and its students' published books were selected among the **Top 100 New Products for 1987/88** by CURRICULUM PRODUCT NEWS and their all-district-level readership.

To obtain a free copy of the CONTEST Rules and Guidelines for your teachers and students, please send a self-addressed, stamped, business-size envelope to: THE NATIONAL WRITTEN & ILLUSTRATED BY...AWARDS CONTEST FOR STUDENTS, Landmark Editions, Inc., P.O. Box 4469, Kansas City, Missouri 64127.

THE 1986 WINNERS

AMY HAGSTROM, age 9
Portola, California

ISAAC WHITLATCH, age 11
Casper, Wyoming

DAV PILKEY, age 19
Cleveland, Ohio

THE 1987 WINNERS

DENNIS VOLLMER, age 6
Grove, Oklahoma

LISA GROSS, age 12
Santa Fe, New Mexico

STACY CHBOSKY, age 14
Pittsburgh, Pennsylvania

THE 1988 WINNERS

LESLIE MAC KEEN, age 9
Winston-Salem, North Carolina

ELIZABETH HAIDLE, age 13
Portland, Oregon

HEIDI SALTER, age 19
Berkeley, California

GOLD AWARD BOOKS

Before initiating THE NATIONAL WRITTEN & ILLUSTRATED BY... AWARDS CONTEST, in 1985 Landmark published two extraordinary books by students. These two books announced our intention to seek out and publish the outstanding works of talented students. And these wonderful books have motivated thousands of students nationwide to create original books.

I read DRAGON and WALKING to my class, and they just loved them! All they wanted to do was draw, draw, draw, and write, write, write!

— Rhonda Pierce, Teacher

KAREN KERBER, age 12
St. Louis, Missouri

DAVID MC ADOO, age 14
Springfield, Missouri